Public Spheres After Socialism

Public Spheres After Socialism

Edited by

Angela Harutyunyan,
Kathrin Hörschelmann,
and
Malcolm Miles

Editorial Assistant: Karen Roulstone

intellect Bristol, UK / Chicago, USA

First Published in the UK in 2009 by
Intellect Books, The Mill, Parnall Road, Fishponds, Bristol, BS16 3JG, UK

First published in the USA in 2009 by
Intellect Books, The University of Chicago Press, 1427 E. 60th Street, Chicago,
IL 60637, USA

A catalogue record for this book is available from the British Library.

Cover Design: Stereographic
Copy Editor: Rhys Williams
Typesetting: Mac Style, Beverley, E. Yorkshire

ISBN 978-1-84150-212-0

Printed and bound by Gutenberg Press, Malta.

CONTENTS

PREFACE

Angela Harutyunyan

The papers in this volume, with those of the companion volume *Art and Theory After Socialism*, originated in a three-day conference – 'The Public Sphere: Between Contestation and Reconciliation' – organized by the National Association of Art Critics, Armenia in collaboration with the Critical Spaces Research Group (since reconstituted as the Centre for Critical Cultural Research) at the University of Plymouth, UK. The conference took place at the American University, Yerevan, between 25 and 27 October 2005; and brought together artists, academics and critics from Armenia, Austria, France, Germany, Turkey and the UK, to address some of the cultural, social and philosophical issues arising from changing understandings of what constitutes a public sphere. The focus was specifically on a post-socialist context for such understandings, while recognizing that this requires reconsideration of the concept of a public sphere not only in the ex-East but in what now becomes the ex-West as well.

Post-socialism does not simply mean a continuing transformation of economic relations, or socio-political and cultural conditions in the former East-bloc countries, then, but is also conceived as a conceptual umbrella under which the disintegration of the social welfare states in western Europe and, especially, post-Thatcherist Britain indicate the advance of neo-liberalism and what is sometimes called modernisation. The term post-socialism offers a conceptually potent challenge to the rigid geographical boundaries and contexts to which it is conventionally applied, and the term public sphere, as defined in Euro-American academic discourses, also needs to be contested and reconciled – or not – with its original Enlightenment theoretical framework.

Against this background, the conference provided a discursive forum for the relevance of, and possible revision of, notions of the public sphere in the context of post-socialist transformation, questioning its boundaries as applied to different historical conditions. The conference's debates frequently addressed the operational aspects of the term and the ways in which it potentiates the formation of subjectivities and identities within the new relational forms of production and ownership which accompany globalization. The discussions encompassed multi-layered and diverse intellectual viewpoints reflecting the interdisciplinary positions of several contributors. The public sphere was addressed as a site for the contestation of collective memory and erasure. The dialectics of historical memory and oblivion affected by the ideological meta-narratives of power were seen to underline not merely the spatial embodiments of narratives articulated by public spaces (such as monuments, symbols, or shrines), but also the temporal dimensions of the public sphere in the post-Fordist era of capitalism – in a way, the public time. Cultural media including art, cinema, literature and mass media were considered in relation to and as public (or non-public) spheres in which a subversive intervention could be made and might realize the potential implied in the structure of the concept. All that is required to more fully explore this potential is to denaturalize the term when applying it to different historical contexts – from the former Yugoslavia or Armenia to Turkey, the GDR, and the UK- and to re-conceptualize the public sphere as a dynamic process, rather than a thing that functions in terms of inclusion and exclusion, or hierarchy and hegemony. And, last but not least, the public sphere was articulated as a performative space in the act of reading, interpreting or commenting through which the embodied subjectivity of the reader, interpreter or commentator constructs narratives and fictions in a way that these identities and relations are acted upon and continuously negotiated. From these debates, two volumes of revised papers, with different emphases, have been produced. In this volume, the material is articulated in three sections: the first considers monuments and the concept of an urban public sphere; the second concerns representations in the arts (including film), and in the built environment; the third looks to issues of identity formation and everyday life, concluding with a provocative essay on the idea of public time.

The conference made a significant contribution to debate within cultural groups and institutions in Armenia, especially in Yerevan, but also to the re-thinking of positions for contributors from the West encountering what were to them new perspectives and shared experiences in the conditions of the disintegration of the Soviet Union in 1991. In the case of Armenia, this political rupture was followed by war and a serious earthquake (some of the damage of which remains evident outside Yerevan). The papers have already been published in Armenian. This volume, with *Art and Theory After Socialism*, completes the initiative begun in 2005, consolidates the link between the University of Plymouth and cultural networks in Armenia (and other parts of the ex-East bloc), adds to a growing literature on post-socialist culture and social formation, and – the editors hope – will aid new understandings of how the conditions for cultural production have changed in the West as well as the East since the early 1990s.

Section One: Monuments and Public Spheres

1

Peace in Ruins: The Value of Mementoes, Temporary Shrines and Floral Tributes as Markers of the Public Sphere

Paul Gough

So Hiroshima. The girder skullcap and empty eye windows of the ruined trade hall. She went through the museum, she read the English captions, and could not believe the cenotaph was so incompetent. The flensed stone and bleached concrete of the wrecked trade hall was much more eloquent.

She stood on the banks of the river with her back to the Peace Park, watching the shadow lengthen across the grey-brown waters while the sky turned red, and felt the tears roll down her cheeks.

Too much, turn away.[1]

John F. Kennedy argued that 'Peace is a daily, a weekly, a monthly process, gradually changing opinions, slowly eroding old barriers, quietly building new structures'. He had in mind not physical structures – such as reverential monuments, buildings and memorials – but social, economic and legitimising systems that might be nurtured and supported through osmotic processes of slow, but purposive, change. It was Kennedy's successor, Lyndon B. Johnson, who captured this ideal when he suggested that 'peace is a journey of a thousand miles and it must be taken one step at a time.'

Such values, however, have never lent themselves easily to artistic translation or interpretation. The language of gradual change, quiet erosion, and osmotic growth cannot be easily converted into traditional understandings of three-dimensional form. This difficulty is clearly evident in the aftermath of the Great War in Europe, a period that saw a profusion of sculptures, monuments and memorials to the dead buried in foreign countries. So extensive was this building programme across north-west Europe that it was described at the time as the greatest period of monument building since the Pharaohs ruled Egypt. In 1919, less than a year after the Armistice, the Imperial War Graves Commission had embarked on a programme to build 1,200 cemeteries; by 1921 132 in France and Belgium were completed and a further 285 were under construction. More than 40,000 headstones had been carved from the quarries of Portland in southern England.

Although the victorious populations, and their leaders, claimed to celebrate peace, their artists and designers found it hard to articulate the idea in visual terms. For most British Empire artists working in the classical style, 'Peace' invariably took the conventional form of a female figure holding aloft an olive branch, a palm frond, or occasionally, a dove. 'Peace' rarely appeared on her own. Invariably she was a junior partner to the more strident figure of 'Victory', and usually located at a lower point on the pedestal arrangement. The most popular visual emblem of peace – an olive wreath – can easily be confused with the laurel of victory.

The popular inscription *Invicta Pax* tells us a great deal about the difficulties of representing peace: it could be translated as 'undefeated in war, undefeated by death, or even peace to the undefeated'. Just as the concept of peace proved elusive amongst the League of Nations, so the iconography of most British memorial sculpture implied that peace was the deserved consequence of victory, not as an ideal worth promoting as a separate or distinct concept. Even those artists who wished to prioritise the idea of peace had to fall back on idiomatic convention. A war memorial designed in 1924 by ex-cavalry office Adrian Jones showed a striding figure of 'Peace' – sporting both palm frond and olive wreath – atop a twenty-six feet high granite column. Jones' approach to the task was, for the time, quite radical. Vernon March's national war memorial for Ottawa in Canada is similarly double-edged. Originally required to 'be expressive of the feelings of the Canadian people as a whole'[2] the winning design was required to encapsulate the core values of post-war remembrance – a spirit of heroism and self-sacrifice, the spirit of all that is noble and great, exemplified in the lives of those sacrificed and the services rendered, so to speak, of those who fought overseas. To the artist, however, the sculpture was intended to have a parallel symbolism. The central arch was a gateway through which young people representing the various branches of the services seek hope, and respite from battle; at the top, on the architrave, were two figures holding symbols of peace and freedom.

During the monumental era of the 1920s, the representation of peace was riven with ambiguity and lacked a convincing visual form. Whereas monument building across the British Empire was widely regarded as an act of official closure, the promotion of peace became the prerogative of pacifist campaigners who focused their actions on war memorials and their rituals. In 1921 the Armistice Day ceremony in London (and elsewhere in Europe) was disrupted by groups of unemployed ex-servicemen with placards stating 'The dead are remembered but we are forgotten'. In following years white peace poppies were distributed in London by the Peace Pledge Union; in May and June 1926 the Women's International League for Peace and Freedom organized a 'Peace Pilgrimage' throughout Britain, which focused less on remembrance and more on the campaign for peace legislation and world disarmament. Little of this political activity, however, impacted greatly on the actual design or location of war memorials.[3]

There is, of course, a fundamental difference between a war monument that purports to encapsulate and define memory, and a peace monument that aims to extend a process, or to further a cause. Inevitably, the issue of political legitimacy is central to the issue of peace: its pursuit has never served the state's monopoly on violence. Because they are associated with internationalism, organizations such as the Peace Pledge Union, the white poppy movement and such like, represent a threat to the nation-state, which regards an anti-war stance as anti-nation.

It is not until after the Second World War that we find examples of public artworks that are intended to exclusively promote the core ideas of peace. These were often prompted by a fear of the consequences of nuclear proliferation. Accordingly, a number of the most memorable pieces are located in such blitzed cities as Dresden, Coventry and Nagasaki. As a designated peace city, Hiroshima, for example, functions simultaneously as a reliquary, a funerary site, a civilian battlefield, and as a locus of political and social debate. Invariably, most peace memorials have taken the form of designed landscapes, preserved ruins and what have been termed 'counter-monuments'. Such approaches to the issues of remembering contest the very assumptions of commemoration. There is less ambition to see public sculpture as 'a terminal act' which closes a period of mourning or martial activity; instead there is a recognition that there is little to commemorate about the pursuit of peace. Not only does peace lack a rhetorical visual language, it is essentially a continuous process rather than one with definable conclusions or an endpoint. Because of this, the iconography of peace activism has largely been developed through the design of specific landscape spaces. As a communal and collective act, it might be argued that gardening has become the favoured grammar of peace. This was exemplified in the 1970s in networks of local, national and international peace gardens and peace parks. They served various functions: in Central America they were created as 'cordons sanitaire' to help promote trans-national cooperation; in the Middle East peace parks have been created as de-militarized buffer zones between warring factions. In central Africa they have been created to erase recent military turmoil and to protect bio-diversity.[4] While not always successful in achieving their goals, such polemic landscapes are intended to be fluid and dynamic, open to negotiation, time-conscious and visible rather than time-determined and invisible. Peace landscapes, whether they be vast spaces in South America or intimate gardens in central London, are agents of repair rather than icons of reparation.[5]

Planting as a form of protest has a fascinating historiography. Even in the formal regimen of the Imperial War Graves Cemeteries there are occasional examples of 'rogue' planting. The practice is perhaps best expressed in a short story by the British novelist Julian Barnes, Evermore. The central character, a Miss Moss, makes regular visits to her brother's grave in a military cemetery in northern France to dig out the 'offending French grass' and plant lean sods of English turf around his headstone. But it was always to no avail: the following year 'the [offending] French grass was back again'.[6] Such acts of vegetative vengeance take many forms and have been branded as 'guerilla gardening' in recent years.

Perhaps the most recent, and most infamous, act of guerilla gardening took place during the May Day marches through central London in early 2000. Protesting against globalism, capitalism and war, marchers not only attempted to reclaim the official spaces but to liberally sow seeds of banned substances and to stain them with irreverent markers, of which the most memorable is the green Mohican haircut placed on the statue of Churchill in Parliament Square. It was not the disfiguration of a state icon that was held to be most heinous, rather that it should be done with healthy green turf, a material normally associated with a manicured lawn, horticultural order, and the 'green coverlet' of official commemoration.

How does this act of violation compare with that other extreme of urban gardening – the mass grieving for Princess Diana that took place in 1997? In little over one week an estimated 50 million blooms, weighing some 10,000 tons were laid outside Buckingham Palace. There, like a floral aneurysm, they burst out of St James' Palace across the state avenues of Imperial London. Although largely interpreted as further evidence of 'synthetic grief' the death of Diana took the major British institutions – the media, the Royal Family, the police and even the church – by surprise, without a pre-planned script, and with few precedents of procedure and protocol. The resulting mass public mourning created a new cultural order. Mourning was focused on London: millions of pilgrims left shrines to the dead princess – flowers, teddy bears, balloons, messages, and other votive offerings. It is still difficult to tell whether this was evidence of a media-induced hysteria or a magnification of normal mourning behaviour. The visual displays of grief, however, are of interest: the ex-votos and material objects of thanks indicate a desire to communicate both with a particular object of devotion and with others similarly affected as well, in a mass event, an outpouring of sentiments making the centre of London like a pilgrim shrine.

In passing, how do we explain, however, the other question that was so often asked: 'Why have we created a cellophane meadow? Why do we leave the flowers wrapped in plastic?' The answer is simple. As one English broadcaster put it:

> Cellophane and ribbons means 'Look, I didn't nick these from the park, I paid good money for them, to prove I care!'[7]

The wrapping provides the necessary context; as all pilgrims recognize the act is more important than the effect.

In creating these elaborate temporary gardens the millions of pilgrims had tapped into a fundamental truth about the linkages between flowers, mourning, remembrance and love. Flowers die. Gardens reveal the actualities of death. Yet the gardener has the skill to nurture and keep plants alive. A well tended garden is a symbolic bulwark against disorder and the randomness that death introduces.

As with any landscape the garden develops meaning through the complex interaction between the here-and-now and the there-and-then. Gardens and flowers are emblematic of the course of human life. Like people, flowers and gardens grow, mature, age and die. The designers of gardens recognize the connections between the individual, the community, and greater causes whether they be religious, aesthetic, or political. Gardens also have an almost unique potential over the other arts. Foremost, gardens act as liminal enclaves withdrawn from the customary disruption of urbanization. In spaces separated from quotidian use, memorials and other sculpted forms are placed under the open sky, in the eye of God where they constitute the perfect opportunity for the elegiac (but also for the Arcadian and the utopian). They offer a new perfection that is at once paradisiacal, and simultaneously transient. And, gardens are linked to memory systems: themes, ideas, and in some cases classical references attach to monuments, including fountains and arches, but also statues. These act as a series of codes that begin to constitute an iconography.[8] Here, however, the garden-as-mnemonic-text is at its most vulnerable, as over time many cultural references will be lost or displaced, and a proper reading will be at the mercy of the linguistic sophistication of subsequent generations.

Proper readings: Utopian spaces in central London

In the absence of an extensive literature on the iconography of peace, the 'City Peace Gardens' project was initiated as a pilot study in 2005. The project had the following limited objectives:

- To examine a selection of sites in southern England with the intention of making a photographic record of selected 'peace gardens'.
- To explore local and regional archives to discover relevant documentation, press coverage and public reaction to the chosen sites.
- In so doing, create an initial typology for the 'iconography of peace' and devise an appropriate methodology for the recording and appraisal of other sites of peace.

The project aimed to create an initial typology for the 'iconography of peace', and through this process devise an appropriate methodology for the recording and appraisal of other sites in the United Kingdom. Many of the garden spaces that were explored through the project were examples of a symbolic landscape of protest – smaller scale versions of those at Hiroshima, Coventry, and Dresden – which often co-exist rather uncomfortably as places of tourism.[9] However, none of the sites chosen in the first phase of the project had been destroyed by war. Instead they took the form of peace gardens and parks whose overarching concept was that they should be both 'a commemoration and a warning.'[10]

This concept became a working reality in the United Kingdom during the early and mid-1980s when a group of London-based architects, planners and environmentalists formed Architects for Peace to work for 'the abolition of nuclear arms and other weapons of mass-destruction world-wide.'[11] It was one of many groups established in the UK to promote the cause of world peace. At the same time, similar groups such as Avenues for Peace, Civil Engineers for Nuclear Disarmament, and the Nuclear Free Zones Steering Committee invited professionals in the built and landscaped environment to support the aims of world peace and disarmament and to work towards designing physical spaces, which conveyed that message.

Amongst the sites chosen as part of the project were two in central London: one in north-east London (the Noel-Baker Peace Garden in the Borough of Islington) and another in north London (the Maygrove Peace Park, Camden). Both sites were developed in the mid 1980s when London was governed by the radical left-wing local authority, the Greater London Council (GLC) led by Ken Livingstone (notoriously ridiculed as 'Red Ken' by the right-wing press, who was later Mayor of London, until 2008). Red Ken was an easy target for the political right – under his leadership the GLC was a champion of unfashionable and obscure causes. It campaigned for cheaper public travel, held numerous community festivals and pursued a variety of radical, but widely popular, measures: sponsoring an 'Antiracist Year', providing city grants to such groups as Babies Against the Bomb, and declaring London a 'nuclear-free zone'. In 1983 the GLC announced its 'Year of Peace' and several London boroughs committed resources to create public spaces dedicated to peace. The sites were selected to serve as a permanent reminder of the Council's commitment to peace and its support for the policies of the Peace Movement. Sculptures were planned, along with an elaborate planting scheme. Opposition was frequent and loud:

> Peace Parks are typically eastern European Government intentions which do not serve the interests of true peace. Transplanting such an expensive gimmick to this country is to introduce an entirely alien and unhelpful concept.[12]

The scheme however had unstoppable momentum. Even at this stage in the commissioning process the iconography of the parks were clearly and readily articulated. The iconography was based on a strict lexicon: poetry tablets set into paths with quotations of peace, a peace grove of silver birch, stone slabs indicating the names of local councils who have declared themselves nuclear-free zones, plants associated with peace, friendship seating at a gathering point called 'the Meeting of the Ways', entrance pergola with rambling peace roses, a sculptural feature representing a crane, and the cherry tree, which continued to bloom through the nuclear holocaust in Hiroshima.

Places of commemoration and remembrance, however, only become an integral part of the public sphere through regular re-inscription. This is most commonly achieved through routine celebration of annual events such as the Armistice or Remembrance Sunday. By contrast, 'remembrance' events at most British peace parks followed a calendar dictated by key events at the end of the Second World War – Hiroshima or Nagasaki Day. At the London peace gardens, peace *festivals* – as distinct from ceremonies – were held annually in August in the 1980s. Accompanied by Irish folk bands, jugglers, entertainers, and – in 1985 – giant inflatable puppets of Mrs Thatcher and Ronald Reagan, the gardens became a focus for dissent and protest of all hues, provided a framework and a site for those espousing a wide range of causes from the scrapping of nuclear weapons to the ending of battery egg farming.

The peace gardens of central London did not long survive the GLC. They remain as remnants of the anti-proliferation movement of the 1980s, stripped of their political origins, and subject to periodic neglect. They do, however, still function as green enclaves situated in larger parklands. Few of the sculptures, plaques, or polemic objects have survived, although there have been attempts to revive and refashion them as accessible spaces. In Islington, the Noel-Baker Garden was refurbished in preparation for the twentieth anniversary celebrations in 2004. The original beds of white roses that had been planted as an emblem of peace in memory of the victims of Hiroshima were sited in a new bed to reinvigorate them and to reinstate the original plan.[13]

Site of protest – Greenham
One of the most controversial of all peace gardens in the United Kingdom is now situated at the heart of one of the country's most militarized sites in recent history. Greenham Common in southern England has been occupied by the military since the Second World War, but grew to infamy in

the 1970s when the US government were permitted to site 96 Tomahawk ground launched cruise missiles under the control of the 501st tactical missile unit USAF. Six large missile shelters were specially constructed to house the missiles; the first to be based on British soil.

In 1981 a group in Cardiff opposed to nuclear power and nuclear weapons set out to protest at NATO's decision to site these missiles. 36 individuals, under the banner 'Women for Life on Earth', walked the 120 miles to Greenham Common. Attracting little attention from the media en route they decided to chain themselves to the perimeter fence of the airbase and establish a permanent peace camp – initially at the main entrance known as the 'Yellow Gate', from where they could espouse their arguments. It was the start of a twenty year protest occupation. There were nine camps in all. What followed is well-known – there were mass protests and huge gatherings – at one time over 40,000 people surrounded the base, and on New Year 1983 44 women were arrested after having broken through the fences and danced on top of the giant missile silos in the militarized zone. The USA left in the 1990s as the Soviet threat collapsed following the fall of the Berlin Wall, but there is an archaeology of occupation that is still evident today.

Since the American military left the site, there have been numerous schemes to both commemorate their role and to counteract the memory of their presence. Inevitably, most of the schemes have focused on how to re-fashion the landscape (although the Common has also become a zone of intense performative activity, bringing together dancers, artists and urban archaeologists).[14]

Since the mid-1990s, there have been extensive plans to remember the recent history of the site. Most of these have been officially sanctioned. They have included a peace garden, a water avenue that symbolically bisected the 10,000 metre runway, and a meadow of wild flowers planted over the old tarmac. However, as yet none have come to fruition. Indeed, very little remains above surface level to indicate the women's long protest: a few painted designs, a strip of tape, some scattered remnants but little more above the ground.

Perhaps inevitably the formal ideas boiled down to a single proposal: a small memorial garden to be planted at the entrance to what is now the business park that occupies the southern edge of the common. Looking rather more 'corporate' than what was perhaps originally envisaged, the garden was realized by former protesters who raised over £20,000 (including a substantial contribution from Yoko Ono) to create and plant the plot. It has two sculptures and a planting scheme derived from the conventional arbo-culture of peace and protest – a modest, informal and low maintenance planting scheme, with highly scented and light-coloured flowers. A ring of seven rough-hewn boulders were brought from south Wales – the home of the first protesters – and one of the metal sculptures is designed to recall the camp-fires that burned for over twenty years. Underneath the calm atmosphere there is some residual anger, which is unusual for a garden dedicated to peace, but perhaps less so for a garden that commemorates an unrequited campaign. This anger is summarized in the words carved into a stone and steel spiral form, which acts as a water fountain: "Women's Peace Camp 1981–2000. You can't kill the Spirit."

At its inauguration, one of the original protesters expressed a hope that the garden, unlike the protesters, would be 'adopted' by the citizens of the nearby town:

> This (garden) is gifted to the people of Newbury. I don't want it sitting there doing nothing. I want people, when they drive past, to go in and sit and dwell on what it means.[15]

Ironically, the notion of guerilla gardening is gaining wider currency in southern England (derived from precedents in north America). Newspaper columnists in 2006 applauded moonlight gardeners (and a wider membership of some 200) who have been 'titivating' roundabouts and roadside verges in south London with shrubs, bulbs and other unplanned regenerative acts. At the same time, artists such as Tania Kovats and Cornelia Parker have been creating transient and mobile green spaces that can be imported into sites of urban blight. Kovats transported a floating wildlife meadow atop a barge from Bath to London via the existing canals and industrial inland waterways. In mid-June 2006 it passed within a few miles of the Greenham peace garden.

In creating these miniature *rus in urbe*, are we seeing another phase in the evolution of the polemic garden; a process in which guerilla gardening has become adopted as urban pastoral, as a form of 'vandalizing with plants', achieved in the dead of the night (as the *Daily Mail* puts it, without apparent irony) by 'comrades in trowels'.[16]

Paul Gough is an artist and Dean of Arts and Media at the University of the West of England, Bristol.

Notes

1. Banks, I. (1989), *Canal Dreams*, London, Macmillan, p. 175.
2. Vance, J.F. (1997), *Death so Noble: Memory, Meaning and the First World War*, Vancouver, University of British Columbia Press, p. 28
3. King, A. (1998), *Memorials of the Great War in Britain: the Symbolism and Politics of Remembrance*, Oxford, Berg.
4. Gough, P. (2000), 'From Heroes' Grove to Parks of Peace' *Journal of the Landscape Research Group*, Vol. 25, No. 2.
5. Hallam, E. and Hockey, J. (2001), *Death, Memory and Material Culture*, Oxford: Berg, p. 90.
6. Barnes, Julian (1996), *Evermore*, London: Penguin.
7. Purves, Libby (1997), *The Times*, 9th September.
8. Rainey, M.R. (2001), 'The Garden as Narrative: Lawrence Hilprin's Franklin Delano Roosevelt memorial', in Wolschke- Bulmahn, J. *Places of Commemmoration: search for identity and landscape design*, Washington, Dumbarton Oaks.
9. Brock, P. (1991), *Studies in Peace History*, York: William Sessions.
10. Mckean, J. (1989), *Places of Peace*, Architects for Peace, Collingwood (AUS), p. 3. see also www.vortex.uwe.ac.uk/places_of_peace/glossary.htm
11. ibid.
12. Anon (1983),*Camden New Journal*, 28th July.
13. Gough (2006), *Places of Peace*, http://www.vortex.uwe.ac.uk/places of peace/about.htm
14. Common Ground (2006), *Common Ground*, www.soton.ac.uk/~kmp401/projectoutline.htm
15. Anon (2002) Newbury Weekly News, 18th October.
16. Hardman, R. (2006), 'Guerilla Gardeners', *Daily Mail*, 23rd March, 2006.

2

STATE ICONS AND NARRATIVES IN THE SYMBOLIC CITYSCAPE OF YEREVAN

Angela Harutyunyan

Since as early as Ernest Renan's article "What is a Nation?"[1] and especially with the development of postcolonial post-foundational theory,[2] historians, anthropologists and practitioners of neighbouring disciplines have become more aware of the ideological implications of the notion of nation as defined in the age of nation states. Postcolonial theory came to question 'nation' as an essential entity, i.e. a fixed community bound by blood, ethnic or religious relationship. Instead, it is a cultural, social and historical construct that can never be fixed or permanent. The formation of national identity, to a large extent dependent upon shared community memories and oblivion of past victories and losses, is an ongoing process. These selective processes of collective remembering, as well as forgetting, require certain instruments and signs to signify community relations. In their commemorative function, serving as a bridge between the past and the present, monuments and public symbols become a tool for selective remembrance, and 'their very essence lies in their relationship to lived time and memory.'[3]

By mapping the public symbols, particularly monuments in the city centre of Yerevan, I will argue that the choice of the symbolic axis in one of the most representative public spaces of the Armenian capital – Republic Square, transforms with ideological battles and changes in power relations. I will argue that signs and symbols are often created and/or manipulated by different ideologies in order to construct certain desirable narratives in the process of national identity formation in post-Soviet Armenia. For my reading of public symbols and their relations to national identity formation, I have employed Homi Bhabha's interpretation of a nation as

Head of Armenian SSR's Central Committee Andranik Kochinyan, showing Brezhnev the model of the Lenin Square in Yerevan and explaining the urban planning developments in Yerevan. Soviet Armenia: Catalog Dedicated to the 50th Anniversary of Soviet Armenia, Yerevan, 1971.

narration where a nation is viewed as ambivalent, 'Janus faced' with its disseminated and dispersed narratives.[4]

Here I have adopted the semiotic interpretation of symbols. Unlike the traditional reading of symbols as fixed manifestations of a given culture, semiotic reading views symbols as signs whose meaning is not inherent within the very visual structure and form of a symbol. The meaning of a sign, and thus, of symbols, when read semiotically, appears to be a cultural construct and is open to reinterpretation.

The Communist symbolic cityscape of Yerevan

According to Jacques Derrida a symbol can be 'undecidable', its meaning never fixed and always in doubt.[5] For such a reading, the very presence of a symbol may also suggest its absence or the absence of signification and the opposite. Contemporary Yerevan is phenomenal in terms of the absence and presence of public symbols which arguably is a post-socialist syndrome as well as a state of 'in-betweenness' of a culture and society.

Talking about present day Armenia, we can hardly avoid the 'post-socialist' attribution. This indicates that even though in the very first years of Independence (since 1991) national identity was being formed as opposed to the identity of the people as *homo sovieticus*, the memory of the past that is preferred to be forgotten, is not left behind. The spectre of the Soviet Union is still present not only on the level of ideology and official rhetoric but its traces are visible in the urban landscape as well. It is particularly manifest in the design of avenues, streets, buildings, parks and monuments. Therefore, in order to understand the symbolic presence of these signs in contemporary Yerevan, it is helpful to make a small excursion into the symbolic cityscape of the Soviet Armenian capital.

Contemporary Yerevan, especially the city centre was designed and constructed according to the plan of Armenian architect Alexander Tamanyan mostly in the 1920s. Inspired by the utopian ideals of Campanella's 'Sun-City', he envisioned it as a garden-city with a maximum of 450,000 inhabitants. The main avenue was planned to form the axis of the city while another avenue, which remained unrealized up until recently, was supposed to connect the main public spaces – Theatre Square (presently renamed Freedom Square) and Lenin Square (now Republic Square). The buildings constructed in the city centre according to Tamanyan's design had both socialist and national significance. While with their scale and function they were supposed to embody the foundational principles of communist ideology, in their form they were a synthesis of neo-classical architecture (especially popular during Stalin's rule) and national motifs of exterior decoration preserved in medieval ecclesial architecture.

Tamanyan's continuing legacy up to the present day and the constructed myth of his figure as 'the national architect' who worked against the grain of the already emerging canons of Socialist Realism, is not only due to the fact that he is the sole creator of the master plan of the city but also of the national form of his works.[6] Nevertheless, it is possible to argue that many aspects of his works manifest the official socialist slogan popular at the time: 'national in form but socialist in content.' In actuality Lenin's policy, to a certain extent continued and reinterpreted by Stalin, was not to repress ethnic or national identities and nation-building processes. Instead, the nation was viewed as a transitional line, a product of capitalism that would be gradually overcome by the ideological and economic success of the Soviet Union.[7] Nation-building processes in many Soviet republics, including Armenia, served the ideological ends of the Central Committee that strived to foster its legacy, legitimacy and popularity in the countries sovietized in early 1920's by the brutal force of the Red Army.

The visual motifs of Tamanyan's buildings, such as the traditional Armenian ornament of wine grapes as well as the figurative representations that were erected afterwards in the form of monuments by Soviet Armenian sculptors in most prominent public spaces, referred to very selective instances of the historical body of the Armenian nation. These plastic representations, such as the statues to the nineteenth century writers and thinkers Khachatur Abovian and Mikael Nalbandyan, were neither supposed to evoke national feelings nor direct the Armenian nation to define its identity as unique and different from that of other Soviet states. Instead, they were meant to remind of the Armenian 'progressive' thinkers who derived their ideological basis from eighteenth and nineteenth century Russian liberal values. These thinkers put their ideas in opposition to the whole body of Armenian medieval thought denouncing it as clerical, dark and mystical. The communist ideology that had its value system based upon making frequent references to classical thought, as well as to the project of enlightenment, encouraged and actively participated in the creation of the iconography of selective 'national and cultural heroes'. In the same manner, the national form of the exterior design of Tamanyan's buildings were there to make the emergent communist ideology, with its newly developing bureaucratic and state apparatus, easily 'digestible' for the Armenian population that prior to sovietization had no encounter with the state's presence in the public space. In the same way, the statues to Vardan Mamikonyan, an Armenian national hero who led the uprising against Persian rule in 451 A.D. and to the protagonist of the Armenian epos David Sasuntsi were constructed as signs of the struggle of the nation for a better future. This was an important component in the official rhetoric of teleological progression from dark ages to the ultimate bright future that would come if the nation adhered to communism.

Even though these symbols still exist in the most prominent public spaces, they have gained a different meaning and significance. Abovian's and Nalbandyan's statues, while still associated with eighteenth and nineteenth century Russian liberal values (since one of the main political orientations in Armenia still remains the espousal of 'Big Brother Russia'), are cleared out from their communist 'dust'. In the same way, the statues to David Sasuntsi and Vardan Mamikonyan are not represented as signifiers of the struggle for a brighter future, implying that its logical continuation would be the achievement of the true communism. Instead after Independence in 1991 they are rejoined by other national heroes such as Andranik and Nzhdeh[8] (whose legacy diminished in Soviet times and any reference to them would be dangerous since they represented the strive for independence) and signify the national will of the Armenian people as an independent nation. The present political regime that came to power in 1998 has been actively playing with this national symbolism, and uses it for its own political and ideological ends.

The Republic Square: battle of symbols
The Republic Square (previously called the Lenin Square) which has been and still is mainly a space for official representation, can serve as a useful example for illustrating the metaphorical and symbolic battle of different ideologies (the communist one and the two official lines that succeeded each other after the Independence) over forming or imposing certain public symbols that people were encouraged to identify with in this highly charged space of representation. Its construction, that started in the 1920s, was completed in the late 1940s, and already in Stalin's time it became a prominent place for official representation.

From the very beginning of the foundation of the Soviet Union monuments and symbols played a major role in shaping the public space and the city landscape in general. They were of a particular importance for the Agitprop.[9] In the early years of the Red October Revolution, symbols created for the representation of the new regime were significant for enlightening society about the new ideology. Most parades, demonstrations and May-Day marches that were so important for the 'education of socialist citizens' were centred on these squares and

Republic Square, Yerevan, 2005. *Photo by Anthony Auerbach.*

concentrated around the monuments. It became a canon that every socialist city had to have Lenin's statue in the city square[10] and numerous other monuments devoted to the revolutionary heroes, party leaders and the fathers of the ideology throughout the urban space. However, the central squares of the city were of special importance in delivering the official message which would be more sound if supported by the leader's image.

Up until the fall of the regime, Lenin's monument on Lenin Square (now Republic Square), constructed by sculptor Sergei Merkurov, served as the main symbolic axis for the square. Despite the fact that Lenin's statue was intended to be the most visible symbol that would dominate the visual field of the whole area, it partially failed to serve its intended function. This failure was due to the large size of the square. The statue occupied a central space only for one part of the square; the one serving to parade military and labour groups that would pass in front of the officials weaving from the balcony during public celebrations of the Revolution-day, the Victory-day of the Great Patriotic War or other relevant holidays. It failed to gain visual domination over the remaining space that evolved around the fountain and was surrounded by the Ministry of Foreign Affairs, the Government House and the National Art Gallery.

With the fall of the regime the statue lost its symbolic significance as the centre of official representation since the communist ideology had already lost its legacy. Being charged

Lenin's Statue in Lenin Square, Sculptor Sergei Merkurov. Soviet Armenia: Catalog Dedicated to the 50th Anniversary of Soviet Armenia, Yerevan, 1971.

politically and ideologically, Lenin's statue was not perceived as a mere image but instead, it acted as the representation of the depicted person; his referent. In this case, any attack on the image or the monument was actually an attack against the person.

After the collapse of the Soviet Union the iconoclastic wave invoked a retaliation against the real man. As Ann Kibbey puts it: 'Although human beings and material objects may seem to us to be mutually exclusive categories, iconoclasm depends on a presumption of likeness between people and objects.'[11] The stronger this identification is, the more the chances of the destruction of monuments and images. After the breakdown of the Soviet Union, the physical fall of the monument from the pedestal came to symbolize the political fall of the regime.

In Armenia the perestroika gave an impetus for raising national questions which found their practical end in the Karabagh movement. At first the protesters who gathered around the Theatre Square saw the solution of the Karabagh problem within the communist ideological framework set up by glasnost. However, as the Central Committee in Moscow failed to address the issue, the movement took the route of a more radical anti-governmental campaign for independence, and demanded democracy. It is peculiar to the situation of many post-socialist countries, including Armenia, that the acceleration of nationalism ran parallel to the demands for democratization. Within the subsequent years of the fall of communism and declaration of independence, nationalism both promoted and distorted the emergence of democratic institutions. The Karabagh war and the militia fighting there that later on would form the army of the Republic, highly encouraged popular nationalist sentiments. Arguments about national identity based on ethnic origins were politically and ideologically charged, serving as weapons for ethnic and political disputes mostly directed against the neighbouring Azerbaijan. The first president of the Republic, aware of the consequences of nationalism for a country in economic, social and military turmoil, tried to promote more universal values of human rights and democracy and declared that 'the national ideology is a false category.'[12]

This undecidedness of the dominant narrative that would reconcile presidential universalism with popular particularism, was reflected in the semantic dimension of the Republic Square. The years of Levon Ter-Petrossian's presidency were marked with the absence of a symbolic axis for the square. While Lenin's statue was dismantled, its pedestal was left empty. The official function of the square was limited to harbouring celebrations of such seemingly neutral days as New Year and Christmas. Nevertheless, once a year the Independence Day was also celebrated here.

While the president's legacy and authority weakened over the subsequent years, the dominant official ideology started to be more and more determined by the military leaders of the war. They had by then victoriously returned from the front line and occupied positions in higher governmental echelons. With these shifts in power politics, the Independence Day celebrations became increasingly loaded with nationalist and military symbolism. The climax of these developments can be considered the military parade in 1996, which with its iconography reminiscent of communist military demonstrations.

The failure to reconcile the president's policy with the nationalist ideology promoted by the military leaders resulted in Levon Ter-Petrossian's resignation from the presidency. The position was handed over to the working prime minister Robert Kotcharian who prior to coming to Armenia, was the first president of the de facto independent Republic of Nagorno Karabagh. Kotcharian was elected as president in February 1998. The new president supported and encouraged the nationalist orientation of the military leaders. Nevertheless, during the first three years of his presidency the symbolic axis of the main representative space for the official ideology – the Republic Square – was still missing. Only in 2001, with the celebration of the 1700th anniversary of Armenian Christianity, a gigantic cross, symbolizing not so much the religious significance of Christianity, as religion as a unifying national force, was erected in place of Lenin's monument. The celebration under the banner 'One Nation, One Culture' ran parallel to cultural, political and sporting events (the Pan-Armenian Games and the Pan-Armenian Congress reinforcing a sense of national unity). The ideology of national identity construction, merged and identified with the ideology of religious identity, was an attempt to overcome the schism between western and eastern Armenians.[13] The political powers used the occasion of a seemingly religious event in order to create a narrative of a united and coherent nation.

After serving its mostly political and ideological purpose, by 2003 the cross was already replaced with a big plasma screen and a mosaic carpet below it, in the middle of the square. This shift of the symbolic axis reflected the favoured political and economic agenda of the existing power structure that combined nationalism with the rhetoric of economic growth and commercialization. The screen, installed in one of the most prominent public spaces of the city, apart from commercials, also displays images of Armenian nature (referred to as 'patriotic landscape'), real-time broadcasts of a wedding procession driving around the square (if the newly married couple can afford paying the price to see its image on a big screen in the very centre of the capital), military parades and marches as well as occasional scenes from the Karabagh war. These images are there to invoke patriotic and national feelings on a medium that, in public spaces in Yerevan, has been mainly utilized for the commercial purposes of advertizing and could be viewed as one of the numerous billboards that have been mushrooming in the city centre since 2002.

Conclusion
Both remembering and forgetting, and the process of institutionalization of memory are highly selective processes affected by social conditions and power relations. The obligation to forget is a prerequisite in the construction of a national present. But the national present of the Armenian nation is not a universally agreed entity. It is fragmented not only for different communities of diaspora Armenians and those living in the country, but also within different generations of a single community itself. Quoting Homi Bhabha,

> To study the nation through its narrative address...attempts to alter the conceptual object itself. If the problematic 'closure' of textuality questions the 'totalization' of national culture, then its positive value lies in displaying the wide dissemination through which we construct the field of meanings and symbols associated with national life.[14]

At the same time this approach acknowledges the 'temporality of culture' and hybridity of the nation as such.

The nation can not be defined only by racial, geographical, linguistic or religious commonalties that are still actively circulated within Armenian academic and official discourses. For Ernest Renan, 'a nation is a spiritual and soulful community',[15] which brings together both the common memories of the collective past and the desire to live together in the present. Thus, borrowing Benedict Anderson's words, the nation is 'an imaginary community' that depends for its existence on an 'apparatus of cultural and as well as political fictions, in which imaginative literature plays a decisive role.'[16]

The nation as a hybrid, constructs its myths; selects its memory and amnesia which are culturally and politically enforced. These myths vary from ideology to ideology and from generation to generation. Due to the prevailing economic crisis, there is a big wave of nostalgia for the communist past, especially amongst elder people. Lenin's image and figure that still has a symbolic presence for many older people in Armenia, gives them a sense of security and stability. Even though the statue itself has been removed from physical spaces, its presence is felt both as a signifier for the 'good old days' and as a terrifying spectre of communism. At the same time the current political regime reinforces certain narratives of historical truth that help to define the nation as something established and essential. This has its political, economic as well as cultural implications. The political implication is the current regime's determination to maintain the status quo power relations by supporting and reinforcing the growing nationalist sentiments in the society. The economic undertone of the 'One Nation, One Culture' slogan is the government's desire to attract investments from the diaspora while the main cultural implication is to define the historical past and heritage as unique and superior while at the same time creating the myth of a united nation as a single body.

This chapter was not an attempt to study how people themselves perceive public symbols and what role these signs play for them. Rather, I have attempted to investigate the formation of identity from the limited and narrow scope of discussing the official narrative. This does not mean that the imposing presence of different symbols in different times was not resisted and challenged through a multiplicity of reinterpretations by different local communities.

Angela Harutyunyan is a curator and critic in Yerevan, Armenia, and doctoral researcher at the University of Manchester.

Notes

1. Renan, Ernest (2002), 'What is a Nation?', in Homi Bhabha's, *Nation and Narration*, Routledge, London.
2. 'Post-foundation' is Gyan Prakash's term for postcolonial theory developed since Edward Said and Subaltern Studies Group. Prakash, Gyan (1990), 'Writing Post-Orientalist Histories of the Third World: Perspectives from Indian Historiography' in *Comparative Studies in Society and History*, vol. 32, no. 2, pp. 383–408.

3. Choay, Francois (2001), *The Invention of the Historic Monument*, Cambridge University Press, Cambridge.
4. Bhabha, Homi (2002), *Nation and Narration.*, Routledge, London, p. 3.
5. Derrida, Jacques (1974), *Of Grammatology.* Baltimore: John Hopkins University Press.
6. For some of the ideological connotations of Tamanyan's design, see Nazareth Karoyan's article in this volume.
7. Buck-Moss, Susan (2002), *Dreamwold and Catastrophe: The Passing of Mass Utopia in East and West.* Cambridge, Mass.: MIT Press, p. 24.
8. Military leaders who fought against the Ottoman and then Ataturk's Turkish army during World War I and the Red Army until December 1920.
9. The agency of agitation and propaganda in the Soviet Union that was established in 1918.
10. During Stalin's rule when the personality cult was flourishing, city squares were mostly occupied with Stalin's statues. It was only after Stalin's death in 1953 and Khrushchev's famous speech in 1956, where he denounced Stalin, that the monuments of the latter were replaced with the monuments to Lenin
11. Kibbey, Ann (2001), 'The Interpretation of Material Shapes in Puritanism: A study of Rhetoric, Prejudice and Violence' in *Cambridge Studies in American Literature and Culture*, Cambridge / New York, p. 17.
12. From Levon Ter-Petrossian's speech pronounced at the session of the Parliament, on 25 April, 1994. http://www.armeniaforeignministry.am/speeches/940425ltp_na.html, visited in 15 October 2005.
13. The diaspora Armenians who emmigrated to Europe, the Middle East and the United States mainly between 1914 and 1921, mostly constructed their identity referring to the historical greatness and suffering of Armenia, with a special reference to victimization during the 1915 genocide. The so-called 'eastern Armenians' who lived in Soviet Armenia under communism constructed their identity with reference to both selective instances of a national historical past and a shared identity as Soviet people.
14. Bhabha, Homi (2002), *Nation and Narration*, Routledge, London, p. 3.
15. Renan, Ernest (2002) 'What is a Nation?', in Homi Bhabha's, *Nation and Narration*, Routledge, London, p. 19.
16. Anderson, Benedict (2002), Quoted in Timothy Brennan, 'The National Longing for Form', in Ernest Renan's, *What is a Nation?* p. 49.

3

Public Sphere as a Place for Gifts: Social-symbolic Characteristics of the City-building of Post-Soviet Yerevan

Nazareth Karoyan

Since the end of the first decade of Independence, Yerevan, and especially the city centre, has been undergoing reconstruction and regeneration. The roads were reconstructed and the sidewalks were changed. At first separate buildings, and then also whole architectural and urban complexes, such as streets and squares, started to gradually emerge. Today, five years since the beginning of this work, the contemporary centre of Yerevan found itself in a new construction rush. One can observe the gradual changes of its architectural features, especially in terms of the proportions, sizes and surfaces of its streets and buildings.

These transformations have generated great controversy. There are major complaints especially amongst the intelligentsia who are concerned that after the completion of construction works Yerevan will lose the characteristics of an open city, its human proportions and harmony with surrounding nature. On the other hand, the sale of urban spaces, and especially the rental deals of public spaces in the city centre create not only aesthetic problems but also bring out questions of private property, human rights, social responsibility and collective life. In general, the expanding construction work triggers a number of other questions. The construction of Northern Avenue is especially central to the debates surrounding the controversy of the regeneration of the city centre. In order to understand the reasons why the matter triggered so much passion, it is important to refer to the primary question of what the centre of Yerevan is and, certainly, the significance and the role of Northern Avenue within it.

The master-planner of Yerevan, Alexander Tamanyan is perhaps one of the most symbolic figures of modern Armenian history and culture. Being among the few artists and intellectuals who reflected upon the urge of one of the most prominent leaders of Soviet Armenia, Alexander Myasnikyan, to repatriate to Armenia, Tamanyan was distinguished with his ability to comprehend the political logic of Stalinism and to translate ideological rhetoric into architectural and plastic figurative forms with great merit. These features as well as the conservative education he received in pre-revolutionary Russia, his practical experience in the field and his awareness of the political nature of the commission, played an extraordinarily large role in designing the master-plan of Yerevan.

The geometrical shape of the plan stretching from the south-east to the north-west which forms the basis of the plan, the grid of rectangular streets running from the south-west to the north-east, as well as the circular streets bordering it from the west to the east in the direction of a clock's hand, came to signify the 1930s enthusiasm for constructing a socialist, just and equal society and reproducing the utopian image of Campanella's 'Sun-City'. However, the mere fact that the city was positioned to face the mount Ararat, and was located on the verge of the valley with a river running through it and especially the hills that start where the city ends, gave a chance for Tamanyan's city to open itself up to and connect with nature. He revised not only the city-building aspects of the master-plan but also its ideological and aesthetic content. As a result, the primary idea of constructing a city that would reflect social justice and prosperity gave way to the desire for designing a garden-city: a place of encounter between earthly and heavenly paradises. This new concept was the reflection of clerical-conservative ideas formed in the eighteenth and nineteenth centuries. Referring to a passage from the Old Testament according to which Noah's ark landed on the mount of Ararat, as well as to the medieval maps of several theologians that locate the biblical paradise in the Armenian Highland this rhetoric attached a special role to Armenians in the history of mankind.[1]

This ambivalence in the concept of the plan had its consequences: instead of modernist principles, the socialist 'sun-city' began to be constructed in neo-classical style. This architectural mirror-image was the sign of Stalinist revisionist politics of the1920–30's. The column and arch system borrowed from the Greco-Roman mimetic tradition which was also devotional in content, came to embody the urban features of a state where the very position of the sun was determined by a single person. The discrepancy between the concept of the plan and its realization was reflected in the functional separation and spatial opposition of administrative and cultural centres as well. Finding an eccentric solution for the first (an ellipse-shaped square, surrounded by government buildings) and a concentric solution for the second (its outline has parallels with the masterpiece of early medieval Armenian architecture, the temple of Zvartnots, which is a three-storey rotunda surrounded with gardens), Tamanyan conveyed dynamism to the plan of Yerevan. Nevertheless, apart from these centres and avenues, the rest of the city centre (secondary streets, alleys and yards) was left unfinished. In fact, the modernist plan was left unrealized. Instead, construction works started on amphitheatre-shaped hills facing Ararat and enveloping the city with the northern borderline that stretched from the east to the west.

The incomplete centre with its administrative and cultural cells, surrounded by newly constructed residential suburbs, came to signify the very void of Yerevan as the capital of Soviet Armenia and reflected the dominance of the symbolic over the sociopolitical. The Soviet-Armenian nationalist rhetoric according to which Yerevan was not solely the capital of Armenian Soviet Socialist Republic but also the capital of all Armenians or the capital of all capitals – a city that embodied all previous capitals of Armenia and was to become the only true centre of all Armenians around the world – was a rhetoric that relied on the very insignificance of the social-political aspect of the city.

The collapse of the Soviet Union and the Independence of Armenia had a paradoxical impact on the life of the city. Economic upheavals, dilapidation of the electrical power system as well as public transportation and communication networks, privatization and fragmentation of the public space caused a rupture in the system of the vital functionality of Yerevan, transforming previous industrial infrastructures into a trade and service-based economy. However, there are still remaining spheres and power structures from the past that preserve the possibility of endurance. Within the cultural- political sphere, the city-building and particularly, the incompleteness of the centre is one of those spheres. The incompleteness of the centre that refers to the past authoritarian communist regime and its historical weakening, has nowadays become a resource that provides a continuation for its representative function, which, in its turn, is being manipulated by the political and economic forces behind the regeneration of downtown and, first of all, the construction of Northern Avenue.

Naturally, this resource is not comprised only of urban-scapes and surfaces. There are other rationalizing rhetorics directed towards collective social desires. Among these is the rhetoric of economic development and creation of new jobs. This was especially effective since by recalling the glorification of labour back in the socialist past, it would also appeal to wider and economically disadvantaged layers of society. Another rhetoric that argues for shifting the urban development from an extensive to an intensive course is meant to secure the support of the scientifically, technologically, economically and ecologically aware classes of society. The third rhetoric refers to city-building: to bringing Tamanyan's plan to its completion. If the first two rhetorics remain unquestioned, the third one is a topic of heated debate: whether the urban architectural significance of the plan is preserved when some of its stylistic and proportional features are altered, or in more general terms, even if nothing is altered, how a plan conceptualized and designed in one era, can be implemented in another. There are even economic and moral issues such as the question of the price to be paid. In order to reflect upon these questions, first of all we must talk about the connotations that were absent because of the incompleteness of the centre, and have been revealed only during the construction of Northern Avenue.

The place given to Northern Avenue is truly exclusive. According to Tamanyan's plan, running diagonal to all other streets of the centre, it was supposed to connect the two administrative and cultural centres. Besides its specific implications for city-planning, it also has a more general one; it signifies Yerevan's role as a symbol of Armenia's cultural and political unity and hence, reaffirms its sovereignty. The axis dividing the city and attached to Northern Avenue with its southern tip reveals the visual symbol of this sovereignty: the mount of Ararat, while the northern tip refers to Armenia's geopolitical orientation of the past three hundred years. Indeed, Tamanyan symbolically attached the plan of the capital – a project of a cultural-political re-establishment – upon the axis symbolizing the expansionism of imperialist Russia. However, the beginning of the Cold War as well as Stalin's subsequent death terminated Russia's political and militaristic expansionism which reached its apogee during WW II. The construction of Yerevan's centre together with that of Northern Avenue was aborted.

During the brief Khruschevian 'thaw' (late 1950s and early 1960s), an attempt was made to convey a social content to the city-building which Stalin's epoch was derived from. The new paradigm of urban construction reflected in mass housing projects, was transferred to suburban areas and would return to the centre only occasionally with the construction of public symbolic buildings (Cinema-theatre Rossia, recently renamed as Airarat, The Youth Palace, The Sport-Concert Complex, The Museum Of Modern Art).

Meanwhile in the 1960s and 1970s Tamanyan's plan reinitiated new discussions. However, this time the historical aspects became the target within which the architectural space was perceived as a bearer of time and memory. There was severe criticism against revolution and historical oblivion. On the example of preserved historical architectural layers from the end of the nineteenth and the beginning of the twentieth century, the evolution and memory gained in significance. Under the influence of postmodernism there were even simple proposals to transfer historical architectural artefacts and re-construct them in a special location and to plan a district that would solely consist of pieces of seventeenth and eighteenth century popular (folk) architecture. As a result, the state took the old constructions of the city centre under its jurisdiction and put numbers on them. In several instances numbers were even put on each stone of the building. Meanwhile, the issue of bringing Tamanyan's plan to its final completion seemed to be dropped from the agenda when the Soviet Union collapsed.

Today, the return to these discussions, as well as the ideas to finish Yerevan's master-plan, are not merely discussions about Yerevan, its centre and the construction of Northern Avenue. In reality these discussions problematize those metaphysical ideas of time and space where the construction of the cityscape is presented as a timeless and total ritualistic-political act, a sacrificial dimension of power and a means to reassert the established identity. Such crisis-driven ideas of space are derived from the fact that instead of reflecting gradual historical developments, these were formed from the necessity of revolutionary assertions.

Within the Armenian context there are plenty of examples of framing revolutionary struggle and social-political aims with ritual, and of expressing them through a symbolic performance. To be more precise, we can recall several examples from the recent past. It is well known that at the end of the nineteenth and the beginning of the twentieth century the Armenian freedom-fighters (hayduks or fedais) had special military dances they would perform before a fight with Turkish disciplinary troops. Secondly, the mass demonstrations of the revolutionary movement at the end of the previous century that started during the Gorbachev years of perestroika, had ritualistic elements (the most famous example, which also gained a ceremonial meaning, was horn toots played at the beginning and the end of demonstrations. This had a magnetic effect on the huge crowd and was to turn the masses into a single body). In both cases these performances aimed at making these struggles meaningful, preventing multiplicity of interpretation and reasserting the legitimacy of these struggles.

A recent political event can serve as evidence. The demonstration organized in front of the president's residency on the night of 13 April 2005 was violently dispersed. This bigger political clash that took place during the term of Armenia's second president was followed by a long series of two-sided accusations and self-justifications from the side of the ruling power as well as the opposition. In its superficial simplicity one of them is significant. A representative of the opposition, in order to prove that the demonstration was peaceful (i.e. constitutional), and that the violent efforts of the government to suppress it were inadequate, announced that people were playing music and dancing during the demonstration. And they were not lying. The demonstrators were indeed dancing and singing. Of course, these expressions of performing arts are only innocent deeds at first sight. The question is not that the opposition supporters were performing in the middle of the night when all law-abiding citizens are usually asleep. Even if performed during the day, the dance would be threatening both to the internal (towards the dancer) and external (towards the ruling class and the power) agencies. However, other questions arise here: who is this dance performed for and to whose gaze is it presented?

There is an expression in Armenian which, when translated into English, would be the equivalent of 'when the cat's away, the mice will play': to do something in a place where the owner is unknown. Lacan calls this the 'other'. The drive to dance under someone's gaze being an expression of both emotionality and openness, at the same time assumes the awareness of the formal frame of the ritual. And this other is the paradigm of Armenia's political-cultural reaffirmation. Every gesture – both individual and collective – and every idea – public or official – is conditioned with the drive to be devoted to this paradigm and to serve it.

For connecting such a diffusion of public and official spheres with a transgressive understanding of historical-political causality, it is sufficient to recall two famous phrases of two prominent British politicians of the beginning of the twentieth century in which Armenia's hopeless condition was reflected. One of them, Lord Salisbury, confessing his inability to stop Armenian massacres, stated that '...Our ships could not climb up to the mountains of Taurus'.[2] The other one, Winston Churchill, after the last conference of Lausanne which was to summarize the results of WW I, simply stated that the last page of Armenian history was now closed.[3] By this he was referring to western Armenians under Ottoman rule subjected to genocide and eastern Armenians who rejected their independence and entered the newly created Bolshevik empire for the sake of their self-preservation.

Before being pronounced by the British prime minister, the paradigm of the ship and the mountain had long become the property of cultural-political forces that wanted to restore Armenian statehood. These ideas were developed in the seventeenth and eighteenth centuries, outside of Armenia, in the diaspora stretching from India to Netherlands and England. The path of Armenian dispersal started to appear in the middle ages. It was caused by the immigration of Armenians living on the plateau and was followed by the invasion of Turkic people from central

Asia to the Caucasus and Asia Minor. Urban areas, deprived of their inhabitants, started to decline. Those inhabitants first settled down in the diaspora near Armenia but later moved on to farther countries and formed diasporas there playing a major role in the political and cultural revival of all the Armenian people.[4] But meanwhile they had to fight for survival.

The survival strategies within colonial conditions implied experimentation with forms of mnemonic techniques (according to Lyotard, 'mourning for presence').[5] From this point of view the rout of the inhabitants of Armenia's last medieval capital Ani is significant. The long lasting wars, massacres, lootings, economic disasters and eventually the earthquake followed by the decline of the state of Bagratuni kingdom, gradually deserted the city between the eleventh and fourteenth centuries, turning it into a ruin. As a result of dispersed and continuous immigrations, citizens of Ani formed a major diaspora in the Crimea. Later they also had to leave the Crimea and settle down in southern Russia (on the shores of the Azov Sea). The roads of emmigration lead their successors to Poland, Hungary and Transylvania. However, the citizens of Ani always preserved the memory of their city and never ceased to be proud of it even when already in the eighteenth and nineteenth centuries most of the diaspora stopped using Armenian as its native tongue and was culturally assimilated with the surrounding environment.[6]

The reasons for the creation of a local identity previously foreign to the Armenian reality can be re-constructed in the oral tradition of popular tales and myths about the unprecedented beauty of the city. Here Ani is presented as an enormous city of strong fortifications, multiple gates, mercenary shops, gifted and skilled craftsmen, deep-minded clerics and brave soldiers. The highlight of these descriptions was the portrayal of 1001 churches with refined stones, high flying arches and luxurious copulas. This comes to complete the visual outline of the city creating sacred and heavenly nimbi for it. Such a sacralized description of the city has two implications about the virtues of its inhabitants. First of these is the *religiosity* expressed in church-building, and the other one is their *devotion* to the city expressed in the desire to keep its memory alive.

Religiosity and devotion had several important roles: firstly they helped to keep the vision of the city alive in a foreign environment and to *survive* spiritually and intellectually. Secondly, throughout time, being presented as virtues, these became resources for the formation of *national* self-awareness as well as cultural-political presentation. This subjective (through self-representation) and inter-subjective presentation (through comparing themselves with the invaders of Armenia) brought about two rhetorics based on genealogical (showing the origins of the Armenian nation as biblical) and historical-cultural (showing that the Armenians are civilized) layers. The first of these referred to the biblical origins of the Armenian nation, while the second referred to its civilized past. These rhetorics that aimed to trigger the interest of European nations towards the construction of Armenian statehood testify that for the cultural and political elite, the establishment of this statehood was imagined as an *external intervention*.

This strategy was a reflection of historical-political circumstances, the most essential of which was the origin and belonging of the Armenian cultural and political elite to the diaspora. It not only modelled their political behaviour, formed the basis for their calculations and motivated them towards activities with different and unexpected, and as history has proven, at times tragic results but revealed the reasons for the formation of various alliances that materialized as a result of external intervention. An example of this was the alliance modelled by Israel Ori in the late seventeenth and early eighteenth century – unimaginable in today's political reality: an alliance with the Kurfürst of Pfaltz, the Austrian Empire Leopold and the Duke of Tuscany.[7]

To understand the inevitability of the political strategy dictated by the intervention of extra-territoriality, it is enough to recall that the first Armenian republic was declared in 1918 in Tbilisi. The attempt to construct a socialist state, which subsequently turned into a totalitarian perversion, in reality was also a result of an external intervention and was imported with the help of the Bolshevik guns of the Eleventh Red Army. This means that the authoritarian system of power is archetypical for Armenian modern states.

The realization of the elitist idea of restoration of the statehood ('territorialization', according to Deleuze) could not be a different type of power than the one based on the acts of gift-giving and sacrifice. During the existence of all three states (the first republic in 1918–1920, the Soviet Armenia and the republic of Armenia since 1991), the power politics that took the responsibility for the construction of the administrative system of the country, had problems communicating with society. For instance, the degree of cultural and political ignorance, the lack of understanding that the political administration of the first republic had to face, is a well-known fact. On the way to forming democratic governmental institutions and electoral systems, the administration had to implement democracy by authoritarian means. The consequences of this dictatorial democracy followed immediately. Through revolts and sabotages they shook the foundations of the newly established state and cleared the path for the Kemal-Bolshevik invasion of Armenia.

With the declaration of independence in 1991, after the collapse of the Soviet Union the transition from the state-based centralized economy to the one based on private property and free-market relations brought about the problem of drawing borders between the private, public and the official. This problem called for an immediate resolution but on different physical, juridical, political and administrative levels: the privatization of land and industry, the creation of the legal code, the constitution of a new administrative apparatus that would regulate the new economy and most importantly, a political power that would organize all these spheres.

Besides all these general problems typical to the post-socialist condition, Armenia had its own peculiar issues connected with the historical conflicts with its neighbouring countries, which revived with a new strength during the dusk of the Soviet state. Arguably, one of the most important internal factors for the decline of the Soviet Union was the beginning of the Armenian-Azeri conflict which brought into the streets of Yerevan a huge mass of people, unimaginable for a totalitarian country. Hundreds of thousands of demonstrators demanding national and civic rights played the role of a detonator in terms of exploding Soviet society from within. Soon after, following the collapse of the Soviet Union the conflict quickly turned into a military clash and an extensive war. The defence of the newly independent state became the prime issue for Armenia's ruling powers, with all its consequences. The most essential was the task to form power structures and specifically, an army. With this specific development, Armenian post-Soviet society was faced with the increase of the role of power structures and nationalist rhetorics. And for those who do not choose means to reach their aims and often refer to the language of populism and demagogy, democracy is the last resort they would recall.

As a result, instead of social and political structures, political parties and patriotic unions based on regional origins and local identities start to play a bigger role in Yerevan. The transplantation of institutions and structures created specifically for the diasporic condition, can have corrosive consequences for Armenia. By gift-giving, ritualistic investment and other practices based on emotional attachment to one's relatives, and intolerance to any kind of criticism in the public sphere, these structures turn cultural-political processes into ethnographic and commercialized developments. These social and political phenomena, termed 'hybridization' in postcolonial theory, are subjected only to the logic of two-sided deals: employing commercial negotiations and cultural translations as dominant practice.

Northern Avenue is the axis of these developments: the purpose of this modernist project that would reveal the vector of territorialization of political rights and restoration of the nation state in the past, is being reconsidered. The first of these reconsiderations is to serve the economic interests of the dominant groups in society and the strengthening of their political power. The second is the re-construction of the economy and the replacement of production with services. Hence comes the objective to develop tourism which encourages the commodification of national symbols. Today, the competition and struggle over who gets to take up the construction of Northern Avenue is a fight between the supporters of the authoritarian modernist tradition of constructing a nation-state and the adherents of the liberal postmodernist project of having a window overlooking Ararat. Can such a confrontation promote the development of a space where private and official are open to each other or will the public sphere be threatened by those malfunctions that exist today? The question remains open...

Nazareth Karoyan is an art critic and curator, and president of AICA-Armenia [the Armenian section of the International Association of Art Critics].

Notes

1. Chamchyan, M. (1784), *Patmutyun Hayots*, Venice: San Lazzaro, v. 1
2. Taylor, R. (1975), *Lord Salisbury*, London: Penguin, p. 168.
3. Churchill, W. (1929), *The World Crisis, The Aftermath*, Thornton Butterworth: London, v. 5
4. Hovhannisian A. (1957–1959), *Drvagner Hay Azatagrakan Mtqi Patmutyan*, Yerevan: HSSR Gitutyunneri Akademiay Hrataraktchutyun, v. 1–2
5. Lyotard, J. F. (1988), *L'inhumain: Causeries sur le temps*, Paris : Galilée.
6. Leo, (1963), *Ani, Tpavorutyunner, Hishatakner, Antsatsn u Mnatsatsy*. Yerevan: Yerevani Petakan Hamalsarani Hrataraktchutyun.
7. Leo, (1993), *Hayots patmutyun, girk erkrord, yerkeri joghovatsu, hator 3*. Yerevan : Hayastan.

SECTION TWO: REPRESENTATIONS AND DISCOURSES

4

Cinema as Political Movement in Democratic and Totalitarian Societies Since the 1960s

Anna Schober

In July 1959 a group of young Yugoslav intellectuals travelled to Vienna in order to take part in the 'VII World Festival of Youth and Students for Peace and Friendship', organized by international communist youth organizations (the World Federation of Democratic Youth and the International Union of Students) in the formerly Soviet occupied part of the town. One of them, the today well-known film director Dušan Makavejev, remembers a very colourful mixture of young people gathering on that occasion: people from Latin-America (Chile, Brazil, Argentina) as well as from Africa mixed with delegations from eastern Europe in their greenish (Hungarians) or brownish (Poles) outfits. They discussed the democratisation and reform of universities as well as the role of the film director in contemporary society and there were peace parades alongside discussion circles about the problems of controlling outer space. One of the highlights of the festival was a concert by Paul Robeson, the 'old, communist, black singer'. But simultaneously, so Makavejev remembers, there was another big concert organized by the CIA nearby bringing on stage no one less than Ella Fitzgerald. Contrary to other delegations, which were taken by bus to the various events and couldn't decide for themselves where to go, members of the Yugoslav delegation, attending only as 'guests', were discussing whether they should attend one or the other of these two concerts. The 'eastern and western world', according to Makavejev 'were competing for the hearts of youth with two black singers, who are both of them fantastic.'[1]

Besides music, theatre and discussions, film and cinema played an important role in this event. One of the two major locations was the Metro cinema, where scientific and educational films were shown as an integral part of workshops and discussions, and as part of the festival an international multi-part seminar of students of the film arts was held.[2] But in this, the VII World Festival of Youth and Students for Peace and Friendship was in no way exceptional: in the late 1950s, film and cinema was employed by a variety of social agents: educational discourses, schools, the sciences, but also by advertizing departments and in governmental information strategies. The art-world used film and its presentation in the cinema-space as media and as a forum to extend their radius of action. Parallel to this, urban movements emerged that inhabited the ensemble of films, projectors, screens and seats in a new way and even transformed them into artistic action in order to create interventions in urban spaces that they themselves mostly viewed as a social and political sphere. And such a diverse appropriation of film and cinema by various social agents happened on both sides of the iron curtain – in a similar but nevertheless different way.

In this chapter, I will investigate the multidimensional involvement of film and cinema spaces in the processes of politicization in both democratic and totalitarian European societies, especially since the 1960s.[3] Therefore, I will refer in particular to the German and Austrian 'Expanded Cinema' and its contest with the 'Free Cinemas' in the 1960s and 1970s[4] and the 'Black Cinema' and its conflicts with state-socialist authorities in Yugoslavia since the early 1960s.[5] These movements were active approximately over the same time span and mutually influenced each other. But beyond this they indicate a historic break in the overall history of political movements in a more general sense: they are an early indicator of a broader transformation towards our current global public sphere, a sphere in which – in western and eastern Europe – media spaces and various kinds of media use, the *mise-en- scène* of public participation, aesthetic style and the volatile staging of collective body-formations, play an increasing role.

Interactions between official strategies and the mobilization of the crowd

The Austrian or German Expanded Cinema and the Yugoslav Black Cinema ('*crni talas*', 'open cinema' or '*novi film*') can be defined as 'movements' because the cohesion inside the collective bodies named in this way – by themselves and/or others – was primarily established via the public activities of their members (members did not come from one institution but had various backgrounds and institutional bonding). Furthermore, the collectives were open, at least to some extent, to attract new members, fans or follow-up groups. So, for example, the Austrian and German Expanded Cinema movement was composed of a quite compact network of artists and film-makers in the German Federal Republic and in Austria, who since approximately 1966 had been in close contact with each other through various common activities and mutual invitation, but whose activities were also involved with the broader student movement of the 1960s. Part of this network for example was the 'XSCREEN' group in Cologne and Munich (Birgit and Wilhelm Hein in Cologne and Karlheinz Hein in Munich), the Viennese 'Aktionismus' (especially Otto Mühl, Günter Brus and Rudolf Schwarzkogler) and the Viennese Expanded Cinema (Gottfried Schlemmer, Hans Scheugl, Kurt Kren, Peter Weibel and Valie Export). These avant-garde activists constituted themselves as a movement also in demarcation and confrontation with the more explicitly politically oriented, leftist cinema-clubs, then also called 'K-Groups'.[6]

In contrast to this, the Yugoslav Black Cinema started in 'Kino-Clubs' – amateur film clubs which grew out of a state programme called Narodna Tehnika, founded by state-socialist authorities in imitation of the Soviet system of youth education. The aim of this programme was to provide the institutional framework, locations and economic means to create spaces that – like the photo-clubs, chess-clubs or the radio-clubs – outside school and other already established educational facilities, separated the youth from their families and extended families and thus led them towards the production of a socialist 'new world'.[7] But diverging from this official strategy, some of the young film-makers started to create products that displayed feelings, observations, aesthetics and a constellation of figures that were incompatible with official ideology. They were supported by some film-critics, script-writers and journalists and sometimes related the activity of film-making with the consumption of jazz music. First, at the beginning of the 1960s, often involuntarily and later on in a more conscious and playful way, they entered into conflict with state-socialist authorities, which resulted in the banning of several films, resulting in censorship and imprisonment, driving some of the protagonists of this movement to an inner or de facto emigration (to France, the United States, Germany). The cores of this movement were the Belgrade Kino-Club and the Novi Sad Kino-Club, but connections also existed to various clubs in Ljubljana, Zagreb, Split and Sarajevo. Some from this movement were later to become prominent film-directors as well as film-writers, journalists, directors of photography and film-editors, such as Dušan Makavejev, Živojin Pavlović, Kokan Rakonjac, Branko Vučićević, Marko Babac, Karpo Godina and Želimir Žilnik.

Besides all the obvious differences – the German and Austrian movement emerged in a more loosely connected process of dissemination whereas the Yugoslav movement created itself inside an institutional structure provided by the one-party-system – both movements nevertheless constitute themselves through, sometimes more explicit, sometimes more informal political actions around cinema-spaces. But at the same time, and this may seem at first sight a bit surprising, not only the Yugoslav movement but also the western ones formed themselves in some kind of response to official programmes or initiatives, as they were also trying to use film and the cinema-space on various levels in order to manage or control a society in transformation. In the case of the Austrian and German Expanded Cinema as well as in the Yugoslav Black Cinema, we can see an interaction between official strategies and grassroots mobilization, even if especially at this point the difference between the democratic and totalitarian context becomes very tangible too.

Already at the beginning of the 1950s, as a letter written in 1951 from F. J. Colligan, head of the US International Exchange of Persons Division, to K. Holland at the State Department's Institute of International Education shows, in response to the youth festivals preceding the Vienna festival described above, American political attention was focused on youth interests in a particular way:

In several overseas countries, our International exchange offices have urged us to develop programs to defend...our ideas...and to counteract the siren songs and sophism of Soviet communism. As you know, in some parts of the world, students become prominent in government and in communal life immediately after the end of their studies. It is important that these future leaders should be friendly towards the United States.[8]

Parallel to this, various foundations and programmes (especially those supported by elements of the American elite, whom Fred Orton calls 'business liberals') were involved in the 'promotion of American culture' via modern art and mass media, whereby the avant-garde in visual arts, music and film gained special attention as a kind of incarnation of progressive American culture.[9] US avant-garde film-makers, who planned to extend their influence, played a role in these tactics. The Constitution And By-Laws of the New American Cinema Group of 28 September 1960 stated that the group was established: 'To encourage and organize international film festivals to introduce the work of the new generation of film-makers in every part of the world.'[10] And in another document of this group's activity, the Introduction to the International Exposition of the New American Cinema (1961 – 1963) it states:

In America, the most interesting things have been happening in the poetic, non-narrative cinema. It is this cinema that we want to show to the world...The young American film-makers represented in this Exposition feel that the official Film Festivals which are mushrooming all over the world have become commercial projects – they no longer show what's really going on in cinema...There is too much emphasis on the dramatic narrative cinema. This emphasis has become damaging. The young American film-makers are sending this Exposition as a sort of artistic protest and manifesto. We are taking a stand for modern cinema.[11]

The first of these exhibitions was presented at the 'Festival Dei Due Mondi' in Spoleto, Italy (1961) and at the experimental film festival in Knokke (1963–64); exhibitions in other European cities such as Stockholm (1964), Munich (1964) and at the film festival in Pesaro (1967) followed.[12] In 1967–68, Adam Sitney travelled with this exhibition through Yugoslavia. 'The New American Cinema' was presented in Belgrade, Zagreb, Sarajevo and Ljubljana.[13] As a result of such statements and this exhibition activity, one of the protagonists of the US group, Jonas Mekas, was described as the 'experimental cinema's own minister of propaganda.'[14]

At the end of the 1960s this expansionist activity of north American film-makers was seen by some factions of the student movement as highly problematic. During the experimental film festival in Knokke (1967–68) for example, students from Ulm, Berlin, Brussels and Paris protested against 'American imperialism in experimental film'. They demonstrated with banners and chants and even became involved in punch-ups with the bouncers at the casino in Knokke.[15] But at the same time the festival in Knokke worked as a catalyst for the formation of European Expanded Cinema groups: most of the film activists met each other at this festival for the first time, and afterwards Dutch, Swiss, Austrian, German and British cooperatives and film forums were founded.[16] Obviously, the film-makers and critics, who formed the core of the New

American Cinema, such as Jonas Mekas, Stan Brakhage, Stan Vanderbrek or P. Adams Sitney, offered a certain discursive framework that gave other film activists, who were attracted by details or particular concepts of the world-views in the American productions, the possibility to create their own, related positions in response to their own, different milieus, a process through which some styles and concepts have been passed on further.

But at other levels, too, one can witness a similar interplay of official strategies and grassroots mobilization. For example, in the late 1960s cities like Cologne started to use art and avant-garde activities to reconfigure the environment of the city in an eventful way and to stage an explicitly modern, cosmopolitan orientation. Since the 'Contre Festival' (1960), featuring among others Nam June Paik, this redesigning of Cologne had an explicit avant-garde, neo-Dadaist character. In the late 1960s the city started to offer artists and film-makers opportunities to organize public performances and spectacles, for instance in 1968 in a still incomplete subway station. In return, the newly formed cinema activist group XSCREEN used such occasions not by doing exactly what was expected of them, but to heighten public provocation by showing films by Austrian Actionist Otto Mühl, which, due to the showing of sexual and obscene acts, produced a widespread scandal.[17] Together with other cinema events staged by the XSCREEN group, the performances of the 'Living Theatre', the establishment of the art fair and several newly founded galleries, this subway event was a forerunner of the later fame of the city as a metropolis of avant-garde art.

At the same time, film was discovered for educational activities: it was used for teaching, for popularizing science, but also as an investigation object in its own right. In universities film seminars were held. Film became a collected item in art museums, and film museums and cinema libraries were founded. Young film-makers and cineastes reacted to this as well. They were among the first to present films in arenas of high culture, to use quotations from educational films in their work and to give the academic investigation of film a different political edge. So, for example, in Austria and Germany in the late 1960s classic US Westerns were emphatically analyzed as carriers of ideological meaning and as exposures of the 'international society game'.[18]

During the 1950s and 1960s, various agents thus intervened on several levels in order to manage the collective being together in a new way. Manuel de Landa has shown that the enormous knowledge in marketing and managing accumulated in the First and Second World Wars was later widely used in a way that military and civilian sectors in commerce as well as in governmental policies often became indistinguishable. And most often the strategies developed in various sectors now used images – films as well as photography or advertizing – in an enhanced way.[19] There were governmental strategies encroaching far into social space, managing health, education, work and leisure-time besides the possibilities of movement and belonging. Then there were the conditions of production and the time, space and body-training demanded by it, the calculations by commercial entities or political parties, local initiatives by the cities as well as the projects carried out by various other collective bodies – art collectives, educational institutions and students' or workers' groups. All these various initiatives together created a multi-vocal public sphere, in which some of these strategies and initiatives combined and mutually backed each other up, and others entered into situations of conflict and struggle.

A similar process took place in socialist Yugoslavia. Here, too, there was a huge variety of governmental strategies, local initiatives of cities and regions as well as grassroots mobilization processes of various kinds. This again led to an unforeseeable interplay between the official strategies and mobilization from below. So, for example, some of the cinema activists used the educational tool of film, in Yugoslavia so widely adapted in schools and advanced training, in order to initiate internationally orientated cinema activities for children that were based on a vision of 'freedom' and 'playfulness'.[20] And at the same time, in Belgrade in the 1960s the members of the Kino-Clubs organized screenings, festivals and parties that, together with the festivities and parades organized by the party as well as by cities or other social agents, gave rise to a vivid, modern and urban entertainment and event-culture. Marco Babac, member of the Belgrade Kino-Club remembers that in some rooms connected with Cinema Rex in Belgrade, a cinema they used for their activities, they organized Saturday-night parties featuring 'not only Louis Armstrong – it was progressive jazz, completely a-tonal and a-rhythmic music.' At some point they opened the window and one could hear the music on the streets:

> ...[You should see these] faces, meeting in...this social moment, political moment and physical place, you know, for me it was a very fantastic feeling...In the cinema club we had pirate copies of modern music and Saturday-evening at this time we were [famous] in Belgrade...Full of young men, we had parties, each Saturday-evening, only with modern music, free.[21]

But, in Yugoslavia, the interaction – or the democracy – of these various initiatives was dominated in the end by the Communist Party, which represented the 'people-as-one.' The party, and its head, Tito himself, held this movable and multi-vocal formation together. As Claude Lefort has shown, through such a final domination, power and society are again fused together and the unpredictability and insecurity that accompanied democratic processes are eliminated.[22] So even if socialist Yugoslavia, especially after the self-management process was implemented in 1950,[23] tried to strengthen collective initiative and collective management at several levels of society, a struggle between various agents, the presence of different positions and of difference as such were also to a large extent precluded. They were only allowed as long as neither the 'people-as-one', the party, nor the egocrat were called into question or challenged, and it was of course for 'the party' and Tito to decide if this was to be the case or not. This led to a situation where on the one hand there was considerable latitude for public action and initiative – of which the Kino-Clubs were a paradigmatic example – and on the other hand there was an absence of public coalescence from below, an absolute domination by the party and a constant need to deal with its non-negotiable decisions.

Various members of the Kino-Clubs emphasized that censorship was particularly concerned with representations of the party, of party-functionaries and of Tito.[24] Dušan Makavejev, for example, remembers that his film *Parada* (1962) was first banned and only passed censorship after he cut two scenes. The film consists of a montage of impressions collected around an official parade held in Belgrade on 1 May , the workers' day. But contrary to the usual representations of such events, one could not see the parade or Tito and close-ups of solemn faces, but various scenes taking place during its preparation. One sees piglets being pulled and sheep carried through urban areas, the painting of official portraits and party-symbols, the display of flower arrangements, rehearsals of young people, an agitated mother, people waiting with empty chairs and facing the empty streets, a boy wrapped in a flag contemplating in front of a shop-window, a Roma band and high up in the air a poster of Marx alongside floating balloons accompanied by the sound of bells. When the film was banned, Makavejev recounts, the censors were embarrassed at banning it and at the same time could not discuss the film. Because if he, as the author, were to have picked out one of the scenes and asked them about their reasons for censoring it, they would have been challenged to explain what could be wrong with this collection of peripheral fragments of real life. So he decided to cut out two scenes, which, after viewing the film another time, seemed to him to be the most threatening: one scene showing an enormous portrait of the then minister of the interior being made based on a small postcard as a sample, and another sequence showing a female Roma fortune-teller in the streets, shouting 'happiness for a dinar, happiness darling' followed by a shot of Tito arriving at the scene by car. With these changes, the film finally passed censorship. Makavejev resumes:

> It was the celebration. And they became nervous, because they discovered that people are joyful without being asked to be joyful, because this was a popular event and not because it was a political event...The main thing was, at a certain point, when you started making documentaries and films you started getting into this zone, that was a kind of grey zone...Basically, as soon as you are in making movies, you're doing something that is not regular, actually art is not regular, art is offensive in any system...[25]

But the uncertainty connected with the irony and the multiple meanings of such films was, in relation to official politics, the party and Tito, more threatening for the communist system than for democratic systems, because the party and the egocrat were installed precisely to exclude any uncertainty and temporariness, whereas both uncertainty and temporariness are constitutive of democracy. In the field of the arts, this led in totalitarian societies, to the emergence of a 'grey zone' dominated by censorship and self-censorship, where actions, gestures and styles are – without any explicit negotiation – always threatened to fall on either the one (passed) or the other (not passed) side.

These political contexts affected the two cinema-movements differently: In Austria and Germany the Expanded Cinema groups constituted themselves in an open contest with other forms of cinema-appearance. They were struggling against commercial cinema on the one hand, and the educational films of the K-Groups on the other, as well as against the ideological corsets of everyday life in general.[26] This struggle led the emerging movements to define their own tactics and to design demarcations and enemies. These approaches were then expressed in declarations as well as in a 'very recognizable' aesthetic style, one which was immediately taken up by the media and so became further fixated and popularized.[27] The Yugoslav Black Cinema also emerged in response to, and in rejection of, certain appearances of film-aesthetic. In Yugoslavia in the 1950s and 1960s, for example, they opposed the conveyor-belt production of heroic partisan films as well as the home-movies made by the average 'ciné-amateur', happy to record flowers and family-scenes.[28] But the movement did not form in such an open struggle since this was exactly what the socialist system precluded. Their cinema-interventions were thus not unified in the same way by one recognizable style and explicit demarcation but were shaped by a constant, but 'silent' and individual negotiation with the party and with Tito, a negotiation which was displaced very often at the aesthetic level. Apart from this, the Black Cinema, like the Expanded Cinema, was a media phenomenon, since it was journalists and magazines that first started to identify various approaches to telling non-conformist stories with unusual aesthetics as something like 'a movement', and who by representing it also shaped and enhanced it.[29]

The difference between the democratic and the totalitarian context is also reflected in the processes of naming both groups. The Black Cinema as a movement was named and identified first by others, that is: by journalists and censors and then by the party and Tito. Marko Babac remembers that it was:

> The Press, I think, the press, all these negative critics...It [referred to] 'not original, it is black, it is only imitating the others, from outside of our country, with strange ideas and subjects. Not original, not domestic, something strange.' In this negative critique, you can see this...blackness...of life...but we never said, before others, that we are black... [this was] never [part of the] sense of what I am, I only deeply felt that I expressed myself, subjectively, expressively, like a foreigner.[30]

By using the term Black Cinema, quite different actions and styles of expression thus became united into one 'movement', which created a framework, to which others could then consider themselves as adherents. In response, the term quickly became appropriated by members of the movement themselves, for example, in 1971 when Želimir Žilnik made a movie called *Crni Film/ Black Film*. In contrast, in the ways they named and presented themselves in public, the Austrian and German cinema activists were vigorously displaying their identification with the American Underground Cinema and the difference of their position *vis-à-vis* other current cinema activities in their environment. Analogous with the 'Film-makers Cooperative' in New York they referred to themselves as 'cooperatives and Expanded Cinema,[31] but also invented adaptations like *"XSCREEN – Kölner Studio Für Unabhängigen Film"*, playing with 'X as in X-rated'.[32] So even if the formative processes of both movements involved a similar fascination, a searching for position, delimitations from other initiatives, and coalescence from below (in response to official strategies and the fixations and popularizations conducted by the media) nevertheless, the democratic and the totalitarian context shaped these cinema-movements quite differently.

A very private public space

Marko Babac, a member of the Belgrade Kino-Club answered the question about his reasons for joining the club:

Cinema, dreams, you know, to run away from reality, from rough reality, very poor...This connection with the dark room, with moving pictures helped me to run into another world, not a world of lies such as in reality, but in lies of dreams. This is something very different. I believe in lies of dreams.[33]

The cinema appears here as a kind of shelter, where one is able to withdraw from the inadequacies of the present: poverty, roughness and a certain kind of deception. This experience was a shared one. Here, in the Kino-Club, one could meet others who had similar perceptions and world-views. There were around 150 people in the Belgrade club, Babac remembers, even if the core was formed approximately by only 25, mostly male members. They came from:

elementary school, high school, the gymnasium, then from all kind of faculties: [law], architecture, technical [studies], more from languages, [from the] philosophy faculty, foreign languages, English, French and painters, students of painting too.[34]

But at the same time, for them the cinema was not only a shelter, but also a place for action: discussions, screenings and parties were organized and the members learned how to make films while producing them, using everything at hand. Through these actions, one could, collectively, rediscover the city and appropriate it in a new way. So, for example, various

XSCREEN, evidence of urbane presence, Cologne around 1970. © Wilhelm Hein, courtesy library of the MAK. Museum for Applied Arts Vienna.

photographs of the Kino-Club depicted the members at various city locations – streets, but also parks or graveyards – with a little camera, posing before it or absorbed in shooting.

For the Austrian and German activists the cinema-spaces played a similar double role of being shelter and action-space. So, for example, the film-maker Wilhelm Hein retrospectively described the search for a place of refuge which at the same time could also function as a laboratory:

> It was as if we were in a vacuum. We were the only ones in Germany making such films. Given that, you're helpless and you have to find a place. First you find such a place in literature, then in the past and then it started with England (the 'London Underground Cinema Festival' in August 1970, A.S.); we went there and located ourselves culturally, but that was not the starting point.[35]

At the same time, and in contrast to the Yugoslav example, the second role of the cinema as an action space was massively promoted by Expanded Cinema protagonists and was even assigned a programmatic function. Peter Weibel, for instance, declared 'action' as the central means of a new art-practice and presented it as 'world-art and independent genre',

Cinema-Parody, still from *Budenje Pacova* (The Rats Awake, 1967, Živojin Pavlović). © *archive of the author.*

...able to claim to repatriate art from the alienated and false circulation spheres (from the studio directly into the museum) to its roots, namely life and people, hence it may claim to have a direct influence on the vital needs of the population, on human reality, on politics.[36]

Consequently, some, and usually the most spectacular actions of the Austrian and German Expanded Cinema, transformed the cinema-space into a site where they tried to act programmatically in order to construct a 'public sphere', to deconstruct dominant ideologies and to use a transformed cinema setting for the building of a declaredly 'different' composition of society. They banked on provocation, on destruction, on attacking the public and on 'art-war campaigns.'[37] And the Free Cinemas and some of the politically engaged ciné-clubs in France in the 1960s and 1970s connected their urban activism with leftist, revolutionary aspirations.[38] In contrast to this, the Yugoslav Black Cinema operated in the beginning with restrained actions that seem in the first instance almost inconspicuous, by concentration on the *mis-en-scène* of love, alienation, sexuality and loneliness and by relating the activity of film-making to the consumption of jazz music. Simultaneously, they transferred their negotiation with the ruling elites on the level of style. Marko Babac:

> I learn, for me, a very useful lesson from this totalitarian cinema, from Nazi Germany and communist Soviet Union. It is [about the] fight for artistic freedom, to be free in creation. How to be free? With language, with style, with film design, a specific artistic style – for example Leni Riefenstahl or Sergei Eisenstein, on the other side.[39]

Acting in this way, the western-European movements occupied very different city-spaces with their cinema interventions, that is not only cinemas in the strict sense, but also metro stations, exhibition and concert halls, streets and squares and even circus tents. The Yugoslav Black Cinema was more focused on the cinema in a more narrow sense, yet combined it, for example, with music as well as educational activities. But even if the performances, concerns, demands and the political environment of these groups appeared to be quite different, they shared a perception of the cinema that involved Utopian sensibilities.[40] In 'their' cinema-space, all of them found everything that everyday city life denied them: freedom and refuge, dreams and communality, orientation and support, bodily satisfaction, origin and the potential for expression and struggle.[41]

In such narrations and practices the cinema emerges as a space where one could, on the one hand, enter a silent conversation between the 'two in one' that constitutes ourselves and the images. In parallel, what comes to the fore is its being a place where the body is relaxed, reacting to the images it is exposed to via film, as well as to other bodies sitting nearby. Repeatedly mentioned, especially by protagonists of the Yugoslav Black Cinema, is also the darkness of the space and the difference in size between the enormous screen and the accumulation of bodies, which in this environment feel small.[42] In this way the cinema appears as a space occupied by intimate sensations – by feelings, memories and inner pictures evoked by those brought there via film – but also by experiences of belonging and of communality.

Nevertheless, through the collective experience of film-watching, the prospective access to a mass-public via film-reproduction and the possibility of becoming involved in processes of stating and exploring the sense of being, this space at the same time also holds the potential for politicization and for triggering political action, which is highlighted so much by the Expanded Cinema protagonists. In sum: the practices of both movements present the cinema as a space where one is able to retreat from the world and, simultaneously, out of which a struggle about the sense of the world could be initiated.

Because of the qualities advanced in these descriptions and practices, the cinema can be called a 'very private public space'; a space for which the dichotomy of 'public and private' is not really fitting. Even so, this does not mean that both terms should be abolished in cinema analysis. One way to escape the usual bipolar division of the world and to be able to make the private and the public qualities of the cinema space accessible to analysis is to complement these with a third term, that of 'social space'.[43] The cinema can thus be characterized and investigated as a social space, where privacy and intimate feelings are involved in a special way and which, at the same time, has the potential to trigger action and so might be involved in the construction of a politically relevant sphere.[44]

But in totalitarian political systems, such as Titoism in former Yugoslavia, this potential of the cinema as an action-space and as an elicitor of a plural public sphere became problematic in a particular way. As already mentioned when referring to Claude Lefort's distinction of democracy and totalitarianism, one-party systems are concerned with eliminating exactly such a political struggle through which something like a multi-vocal public sphere could be called into being. In former Yugoslavia this was even more complicated as, since 1950, a self-management system had been implemented that strengthened initiative and collective action even when the system was at the same time concerned that such action and initiative should not accumulate into a political opposition. Here we again encounter the grey zone mentioned above, controlled by censorship and non-negotiable party-decisions. But inside this grey zone in such one-party-systems – as these cinema movements show – the actions around urban spaces could also initiate something like a movement that involved others, created discourse, triggered discussions in newspapers, magazines and public places and challenged the ruling authorities. So the strict distinction advocated by Claude Leford between democratic and totalitarian societies regarding the possibilities of an emergence of a political public sphere also needs to be questioned,[45] and it can be shown that in state-socialist societies like Yugoslavia non-conformist movements emerged that formed something that one can call, for example, the informal public sphere.[46]

Here, too, the overall handling of 'privacy' and 'public' was not the same in democratic and totalitarian societies, and especially the meanings of 'private' were re-envisaged in the 1960s. In democratic, capitalist societies, 'private' is usually associated not only with the spheres of families and intimate relations but also with private markets and individual initiative. Several of these meaning-clusters have now been seriously questioned by the student movement and by an emerging feminism, which have shown that 'the private is political', have made sexuality and the body a highly discussed issue, have challenged the 'nuclear family' and have at the same time struggled for collective grassroots democratic control of production and distribution and for communality in general. And in parallel, as already mentioned, the welfare-states extended their area of influence and management far into the 'private' realm of family, sexuality, health, child-care, the body, etc., and in doing so have subjected the areas of production, commerce and consumption to new regulations too. These areas of life have thus already become politicized and opened up to discourse by state attempts to manage them, something to which other collective agents have now responded with other political positions.[47]

In state-socialist societies, on the other hand, the private sector and privacy were regarded by the authorities with general suspicion and were subjected to repression, control and even destruction. So, for example, the regimes tried to push back the influence of the churches and of families and clans in general, but especially in the field of education.[48] They transferred private estates to state property to a large extent and 'love' became in official discourse closely connected with the people, the party and the egocrat himself.[49] It was precisely because of this general suspicion hanging over anything 'private' that the focus of some of the protagonists of the Black Cinema on love, sexuality, intimacy and sensuality had such a politically explosive force. And vice versa, the enormous importance that the regime invested in everything official and the over-visibility of the party and the egocrat made the 'private-public' space of the cinema so attractive to young people in search of meaning and sense.

At this point, the Expanded Cinema meets closely with the activities of the Black Cinema, even if their actions were triggered by different political circumstances. The protagonists of this movement in Cologne or Vienna acted in tune with the student movement by being concerned with a political view of the 'private', with the proclaimed abolition of the nuclear family, with the questioning of sexual taboos and with the promotion of public action in this respect.[50] In doing so they too seem to turn attention onto the cinema, because by its very quality of being a very 'private-public' space it helped to expose precisely these intimate issues and to turn them into politically relevant questions.

Conflicts, violence and the exhibition of the excluded

Karpo Godina worked as a cameraman in several Black Cinema productions, but was also a member of one of the Ljubljana Kino-Clubs and made several films as a director until he was banned from that function in 1972. He remembers a violent action precipitated by one of the films for which he was doing the photography. *Rani Radovi/Early Works* (Želimir Žilnik, 1969), a film which already in its title referred to a seminal work by Karl Marx, was successfully defended by Želimir Žilnik before the court with the argument that the film, by posing questions about sense and self-sovereignty, was not attacking the current socialist system but only wanted to advance it. Nevertheless, during a projection of the film in Kruševac, Serbia, former partisans, who were among the public, started to shoot at the screen.[51]

Another episode, this time in Munich in 1968 as part of the cinema-action *Exit* by Peter Weibel, shows quite plainly the difference between the two movements. In a small cinema in Schwabing, he and some other activists attached rockets and fire-crackers to a screen made of silver foil.

During the projection they were fired and flew fizzling, smoking and sparkling towards the public. At the same time the artist spoke through a megaphone about the aggression of the state and of society against the individual. The public fled the room or hid behind seats and pillars and the next day newspapers posed headlines like 'Warum schiessen sie nicht auf das Publikum?' ('Why don't you shoot at the audience?').[52]

In Yugoslavia, the aggression and confrontation in which *Rani Radovi* became involved, was carried out by members of the party and the political system in general, while the Expanded Cinema itself was strongly orientated towards a confrontational relationship to the public. The Black Cinema quite often came into conflict with the state-socialist authorities, because the directors raised issues and/or showed something in their films that, in this environment, otherwise was not supposed to be portrayed. And by presenting fragments and traces of what usually was excluded or neglected, their productions triggered collisions of images, judgements and beliefs that led in return to heated discussions and fervid fascination-stories, but also to acts of censorship, reinforced control, exclusion, banishment and expatriation. In this respect, in this chapter I can only start to present some examples and initial considerations.

Since the state-socialist system, as already mentioned, precluded or at least heavily monitored any form of conflict and struggle, both became issues that some films enhanced and portrayed.[53] One of the most provocative and because of this immediately forbidden films (until 1990) was *Plastični Isus/Plastic Jesus* (Lazar Stojanović, 1971), which led to its author going to jail between 1972 and 1975. Through various kinds of found-footage material, but also some self-produced sequences, the film presented quite a wide spectrum of usually strictly forbidden topics: one could see Nazi songs and extracts from Hitler speeches as well as Ustaša fighters or Croatian emblems. In addition, in the last part of the film the main character is carrying a gun and shooting at dead victims of massacres happening during the Second World War, or he is depicted as watching a sex film while acting as a baby-sitter for a young girl. In the course of the film he comes into increasing confrontation with his environment and towards the end he is shown retreating into the countryside, shooting around without obvious reason and with his shaven head, black jeans and black undershirt, gun in hand, looking to today's eyes like an early version of one of the warlords who surfaced in ex-Yugoslavia in the 1990s.[54]

Some films like *Grad/The City* (Živojin Pavlović, Marko Babac, Kokan Rakoniac, 1963) or *Nemirni/Restles* (Kokan Rakoniac, 1967), show youth-groups trapped in loneliness, love, alienation, boredom, loss of meaning, excess and aimlessness. Other productions, for instance, *Budenje Pacova/The Rats Awake* (Živojin Pavlović, 1967), portray prostitution, pornography, unemployment and everyday police spying in an environment of mud and poverty. In doing so, these films present everyday city life in Belgrade quite plainly affected by experiences and issues that were officially threatened as 'conquered' and 'bourgeois'.

Besides struggle and conflict, any emergence of difference (between ethnic and religious groups, political differences, gender difference, social deviance etc.) inside the collective body called 'Yugoslavia' was also something that the socialist regime closely monitored and tried to suppress as much as possible – for instance with the slogan *brastvo i jedinstvo* (brotherhood and unity), which represented unity and non-antagonistic, amicable relations among the 'brothers'. The only difference allowed was that *vis- á- vis* other political systems (capitalist, imperialist, Stalinist). In reaction to this overall suppression, directors who were officially labelled as being 'black' focused quite frequently on the representation of the aberrant, the abnormal and unusual. The already-mentioned film *Budenje Pacova*, for example, opens with a sequence depicting a choir rehearsal, during which, suddenly, one of the members starts singing her own melody and sticks to it even after having been reproved by the conductor, so that the rehearsal has to be terminated. But also in cineaste discourse, (national) differences between the Croat, Serbian and Slovenian productions became an issue. After the Pula Film Festival in 1969, the film critic Slobodan Novaković started a discussion about different national 'film languages' and different aesthetic traditions in the well-known journal Filmska Cultura.[55] Since this was, even before the Croatian uprising in 1971, one of the most threatening issues in former Yugoslavia, the party immediately stopped him from discussing the topic and he had publicly to recant the theses he had developed around it.

Nevertheless, difference, as well as conflict, was not represented only as part of the film narration, but was usually transferred at an aesthetic level too. To mention only one example: *Čovec nije Tica. Ljubavni Film/Man is not a Bird. A Film Romance* (1965) was an early film by Dušan Makavejev, which explored difference specifically via a representation of tactility. The camera repeatedly lingers on 'hairy' surfaces and in this way makes unusual correspondences between various objects depicted almost tangible. In several sequences one sees close-ups of the soft, blond, wavy hair of Raika, the female protagonist (Milena Dravić), which she is sometimes also brushing or shaking in front of the camera. In the love-sequences one sees the lovers naked under an unusual, dark, hairy bedcover. The hair theme is further accentuated by an old, peasant hair-collector, who at a certain point enters the hairdresser's saloon where the female protagonist works, takes some hair out of the bin and, in passing, reaches deep into the blond hair of the protagonist. Together with the light, showing sometimes extreme contrasts of darkness and luminosity, these tactile details bestow an enhanced erotic dimension on the film that somehow doubles the erotic vibrancy of the female protagonist, played by Milena Dravić. During this period in Yugoslavia she was perhaps the actress most in demand, both by directors as well as by the public. In this way, tactile difference underscores sexual difference and vice versa. This is an interplay that emerges in other films too.

Peter Weibel, attack lecture, underground explosion, 1969 Munich. © *Peter Weibel.*

By representing on several film-levels something that was usually not seen, was excluded, neglected, downplayed or ignored, the Black Cinema productions touched the raw nerves of the Yugoslav collective constitution. Nevertheless, the motivations for such representations inside the group were also quite diverse. Dušan Makavejev, for instance, insists that Black Cinema activists 'fought for differences in order to bring the party to be more what their programme says.'[56] Others, in contrast, were more concerned to develop an essayistic, existentialist style in order to oppose totalitarianism on an aesthetic level.[57] But despite this, all of their productions were looking for adherents among members of the public and were, via stories and aesthetic tactics, trying to seduce them. Because of the multi-dimensional reception-stories that their productions triggered, involving fascination and involvement as well as censorship, control, banishment and expatriation, they can today, retrospectively, because of their status of being formerly banned or considered as a taboo, be read as bearers of something that was later to develop into an enormous explosive political force.

Members of the kino-club Beograd shooting *Metamorfoza* (1955). © *Kinoteka Yugoslavia, Belgrade*.

As already mentioned, Expanded Cinema activists, on the other hand, oriented their performances much more explicitly towards challenging and attacking the 'instruments of domination, which bind the individuals to the values, goals, and norms of the state.'[58] This approach also sometimes resulted in aggressive acts towards the public. This becomes evident, for example, in connection with the 'flagellations of the public' that the artists Peter Weibel and Valie Export conducted in 1968 as part of the festival Underground Explosion in Munich 1968, where they threw barbed wire at the audience. But at the same time, and as part of their oppositional political position, Expanded Cinema productions also portrayed, what in their environment, was considered to be non-representable or taken as a taboo; for example with respect to sexuality, corporeal shame, religion or attitudes towards the Second World War and fascism. The film 6/64 Mama und Papa/Mum and Dad (Kurt Kren, 1964) of the homonymous action by Otto Mühl, showed a fast-cut montage of close-ups of a naked female body, lying on a table being encased with earth, flowers, and pigment, rubbed in with a sperm-like substance, wallowing in mud and slime, and subjected to various obscene gestures by the male artist. As well as underground films and Expanded Cinema productions, Birgit and Wilhelm Hein started showing porn films, bought in Scandinavia and which were officially forbidden in Germany until 1975, as part of their Cologne cinema programme in the early 1970s.[59]

A two-minute short film, again by Kurt Kren, Schatzi/Darling (1968), shows the calculated breaking of taboos with which several Expanded Cinema productions were concerned in a paradigmatic way. The film confronts viewers with a single photograph showing a tall man in uniform from behind watching over the field in front of him which is covered by dense piles of corpses. The film does not let one see the photograph immediately. At first one sees a montage of almost abstract, flickering, darker and lighter coloured grey planes, which can only slowly be identified as blurred shots of the same image. Only in the second part of the film do these images flash up more sharply for a second. As viewers of the film, we are placed in a similar position in relation to the corpses as the man shown in the photograph – we somehow gaze over his shoulders. The image appears too briefly to be able to make an accurate historical identification, yet the mass of corpses and the posture of the man in uniform suggest that we are confronted with a concentration-camp photograph. But what the photograph primarily presents is the standing man gazing at the dead bodies, a gaze that is thus directed at something – death. In modern western societies death is not usually portrayed directly and is generally placed beyond the borders of the legitimate. For us, as the film's audience, by occupying a similar position as the viewer in the picture, i.e. by being encouraged to gaze so to say 'with his eyes', our own gaze, slowly penetrating the grey fog, somehow also becomes characterized as transgressing a taboo. The irritating title of the film Schatzi/Darling further enhances this enacted parallel between different – pornographic, obscene, de-legitimate – forms of transgressive gazing[60] since it relates the concentration-camp photograph to a pet name used widely in everyday love-relationships. 'Schatzi', in Austria is quite commonly the name of an object of sexual desire, yet here it is violently placed in another context. This displacement evokes the feeling that the relation between gazer and the object in the photograph could also involve lust and desire and is characterized by a hierarchy. Consequently, even if the photograph is too blurred to be able to decode the nationality or the military grade of the beholder, he is

"Hairy" correspondences, still from Čovec nije Tica.
Ljubavni Film (*Man is not a Bird. A Film Romance* 1965,
Dušan Makavejev). © *archive of the author*

usually identified as an SS officer.[61] The title *Schatzi* with its sexual and erotic associations becomes something that might possibly, at first blurred and cryptically so, but then also clearly noticeably and in a flash, be connected with fascism. It might be deduced from this that every sexual relationship could be suspected of being related to fascism. These ideas were expressed at the same time in Germany in the 1960s through discourses which closely related the repression of the sexual drive to racist and anti-Semitic evisceration.[62] In this logic, actions referring to sexuality in a much more radical way, such as those carried out by Viennese Actionism and Expanded Cinema can also be related to the fascist past. The question of how such a connection should be interpreted in the film by Kurt Kren certainly remains open. While this film deals explicitly with the fascist past, most of the other Expanded Cinema actions, in contrast, rather used the interspersion of single references to Auschwitz, the SS or *Wehrertüchtigung* in order to characterize their deeds violating sexual taboos simultaneously as *per se* anti-fascist and politically progressive. But in doing so, they aroused protest and public discourse as well as linking-up-processes with other positions, eager to 'free' humanity in general via sexuality, and thus participated in reshaping the aesthetic-political regime of the 1970s.[63]

So both movements' productions and interventions touch on what otherwise, in the milieus they were working in, was considered to have been either abolished and overcome, such as 'deformations' of the conquered capitalist societies (in Yugoslavia), or what was simply excluded as 'obscene', 'pornographic' or 'offensive' (in western society and Yugoslavia). The Yugoslav movies achieved this by calculating the reactions of the one-party-system and by simultaneously seeking accomplices and sympathizers among the public, whereas the Expanded Cinema achieved a similar effect by measuring and considering a provocative, shocking effect on the public and by simultaneously establishing visible demarcations vis-à-vis other aesthetic and political positions. In this way, both were involved in plural reception-histories and participated in the double-edged re-definition of the political and aesthetic landscape from which they emerged.

Dispersal, anticipation and follow-up groups

In the 1960s, out of the polyphonic mingling of social city-spaces in Belgrade, Vienna and Cologne, movements emerged that occupied instants, places, issues and occasions. They constituted themselves as politically relevant agents, temporarily transforming social space into a 'public sphere' (western Europe) and an 'informal public sphere' (eastern Europe). Several characteristics of these movements indicate a change in the overall history of political mobilization, which unites them with the broader student movement of 1968 too. All of them show that

Photographic flash, still from *Schatzi* (Darling, 1968, Kurt Kren). © *archive of the author*

politicization processes no longer occur mostly in the spaces of political parties and their youth organizations – and do not even have to be connected with such spaces or with "politics" in a narrow sense at all. Instead, they are happening in cultural spaces, in the bedrooms, as well as on the streets. They are connected to the most private, intimate feelings, sensations and issues and have led to the development of temporary collective bodies that made themselves visible through certain aesthetic styles and by relating to the media in a particular way.

But both Expanded Cinema as well as Black Cinema were short-lived movements, even if at the same time, they in a certain sense still exist today through fascination-histories, allusions and link-up-processes. Already by the mid-1970s both movements had started to disperse. In 1973 for example, Dušan Makavejev and Želimir Žilnik went to the airport and left the country, since 'it came close to jail.'[64] Lazar Stojanović was arrested and put in prison between 1972 and 1975. Others continued to work, but in related fields, or went to work in other parts of the country. So for example, Karpo Godina worked as a cameraman but could not work as a director in Slovenia until the 1980s, and Marco Babac was mainly engaged as a cinema editor and as a teacher in the Belgrade film-school.[65]

A similar erosion process was taking place in western Europe: in 1974 Otto Mühl and the commune formed around him went to live in the countryside in Austria.[66] At the same time, Valie Export became more involved in feminism and started to work mainly on her own.[67] Peter Weibel became a teacher, musician, curator and author.[68] Wilhelm and Birgit Hein conducted several programme cinemas in Cologne and in the early 1980s, disappointed by their experiences in the field of art in a more narrow sense, started to work mainly as performers with live theatre actions in close collaboration with the audience.[69]

In the 1980s, discussion around post-modernity raised a strong critique of the dogmatism of the avant-garde, which led some of the protagonists, as well as outside observers of the movements, to reflect differently upon their previous work. At the same time, the cinema space has itself become transformed. In some cases it has become less dark and has mutated into a video and computer space where films are seen as one mode of communication and entertainment amongst others. Since the 1990s in eastern and western Europe, neo-avant-garde movements have emerged that occasionally have close links with their ancestors from the 1960s. They call themselves Kinoki (Vienna), Kinoapparatom (Zurich) or Illegalni Bioskop (Illegal Cinema, Belgrade). The fall of the iron curtain, the disintegration process and war in former Yugoslavia, and the several efforts made in managing a fresh 'growing together' of the eastern and western world, for a short time attracted international attention to aesthetic and artistic developments in these regions, which led also to the current renewed interest in the movements of the 1960s.

One example can be mentioned as perhaps being particularly significant for the *longue durée* of collective memory tied up to cinema spaces. In the course of the protest movements against Slobodan Milošević, one space in Belgrade became a kind of shelter and expansion point for the movement and the various cultural activities they triggered: the Cinema Rex. Exhibitions, discussions, rehearsals, and video presentations, as well as theatre performances, were hosted. Interestingly, the Cinema Rex was never really a cinema. It was erected as a Jewish cultural centre in the beginning of the twentieth century and later became a location for several party activities. Only in the 1980s was it 'dressed up' as a cinema in the course of a film shoot, and it was later adapted as a cultural centre by various oppositional groups. Perhaps they kept the name Cinema Rex because in Belgrade in the 1960s there had already been a Kino-Club cinema of the same name and acting, as we have seen, in a similar way as a home for progressive, spectacular cultural activity. This, again, could be taken as evidence that the interventions of the 1960s still have an evolving force today and can sometimes perhaps trigger renewed political deeds.

Anna Schober is a researcher in film studies at the University of Vienna.

Notes

1. Interview with Dušan Makavejev, October 4 2007.
2. RFE (Radio Free Europe) Background Report 15 July 1959, "E" Distribution 170. Open Society Archives Budapest, Box 95-2-174.
3. This essay presents the framework and first theses of the research project: *City Squats – The cinema as a space for political action,* currently financed by the *FWF. Austrian Science Fund* (2006–2009).
4. Schober, Anna. (2006), Political Squats: Cinema and City as Movers of the Real' in: Christian Emden, Catherine Keen und David Midgley (eds.), *Imagining the City,* Volume 1, Oxford et al, pp. 249–271.
5. Goulding, D. (2002) *Liberated Cinema. The Yugoslav Experience 1945–2001,* Bloomington and Indianapolis, (espec. 59f. and 66f) and Marko Babac, *Kino-Klub "Beograd",* Belgrade 2001.
6. Interview with Birgit Hein, December 4 2004.
7. Babac, Kino-Klub "Beograd", 2001, 74ff,
8. NARA 80.4614/6-1351.Quoted in Kotek, J. (1996) *Students and the Cold War,* Oxford, p. 201.
9. Fred Orton. (1996), Footnote One: 'The Idea of the Cold War', in Orton, Fred., & Pollock, G., (eds.), *Avant-Gardes and Partisans Reviewed,* Manchester, 205–218.
10. See: Austrian Film Museum Vienna, Documentation department, Anthology archival-material, Dossier: New American Cinema, file 1 (1960).
11. See: Austrian Film Museum Vienna, Documentation department, Anthology archival-material, Dossier: New American Cinema, file 1 (1963).
12. Hein, Birigit. (1971), *Film im Underground,* Frankfurt/ Main, Berlin, Vienna, 72 and 122f.
13. Conversation with Branko Vučićević, October 10 2007.
14. Banes, Sally. (1993), *Greenwich Village, 1963: Avant-Garde Performance and the Effervescent Body,* Durham, p. 173.

15. Reitz, Edgar. (1968), 'Parolen, Proteste, Pornographie. Ein Brief' in: *Film*, February, pp. 17–18.
16. Hein, Birigit (1971) *Film im Underground*, Frankfurt/ Main, Berlin, Vienna, 133 and 136f.
17. This is documented in: Hein, Wilhelm and Birigit., Michelis, Christian., Wiest, Rolf. (ed.), (1971) XSCREEN. *Materialien über den* Underground-Film, Cologne, 116.
18. For example in: Alexander, Georg. (1967) 'Filme wie aus Beton. Western – das internationale Gesellschaftsspiel.' In: *Film*, December 14–20. Westerns were also shown and discussed at the leftist 'Freies Kino' (free cinema) in Vienna in the early 1970s. See: Interview with Dieter Schrage, co-founder of the *Freies Kino*, February 10 2004.
19. de Landa, Manuel. (1991) *War in the Age of Intelligent Machines*, New York, pp. 5 and 11.
20. Dušan Makavejev was invited as Yugoslav delegate to the 'film and youth sub-commission' of the communication department of Unesco. There they picked up a tactic of involving children in active film-making developed already by a Catholic priest in Italy and took this as model for an international network of bringing children into film-making, which resulted in an international annual competition. As a result, 30 to 40 children's cinema-clubs rapidly spread throughout Yugoslavia and a lot of film-makers started to work in children's education programmes. Interview with Dušan Makavejev, October 4 2007. The film *Nova Igračka/The New Toy* (1964) by Makavejev documents this work with children.
21. Interviews with Marko Babac, February and March 2004.
22. Lefort, Claude.(1996), 'The Image of the Body and Totalitarianism' In: Lefort, Claude. (1996) *The Political Forms of Modern Societies. Bureaucracy, Democracy, Totalitarianism,* Cambridge and Oxford, 292–306, 297f.
23. The implementation of self-management was aimed at decentralization and a gradual withering away of the state and installed worker's councils as basic economic units and local governmental bodies of the commune as central political units. Nevertheless, the commune remained a central party organ through which the Central Commitee of the Communist Party could exercise control. Harold Lynn on the processes of forming a new elite, which happened immediately: 'The local party members, who control the communes, soon tended to identify themselves with the managers running the local enterprises', something, which 'gave rise to what the Yugoslavs call 'localism', or 'particularism'.' See: Lydall, Harold. (1984) *Yugoslav Socialism. Theory and Practice*, Oxford, 71f.
24. Interviews with Marko Babac, February and March 2004.
25. Interview with Dušan Makavejev, October 4 2007.
26. The film-maker Birigit Hein, who with Wilhelm Hein and others in 1968 founded the alternative XSCREEN projection space in Cologne, described the explicitly politically engaged cinema-movements as 'ignorant' regarding 'formal innovative art' and accused them of a simplistic 'one-to-one ideology', which for example seeks to rouse people against war by showing a dying soldier. See: Birigit Hein in an interview in Beyerle, Mo., Brinckmann, Noll., Gramann, Karola., Sykora Katharina. (1984) 'Ein Interview mit Birigit Hein' *Frauen und Film* 37 (Avantgarde und Experiment), pp. 95–101, 96.
27. Important for this were major magazines, for example *Der Spiegel*, as well as the local press; but television was also very influential, since it showed special programmes on the movement.
28. Interviews with Marko Babac, February and March 2004. And: Interview with Dušan Makavejev, October 4 2007.
29. In 1969 the magazine *Borba* published a supplement on the 'crni talas' and articles on the movement regularly appeared in *Filmska Kultura*.

30. Interviews with Marko Babac, February and March 2004.
31. See the conversation of Wilhelm and Birigit Hein with collegues in 1967 and 1968 reprinted in: Habich, Christiane., Hein, Wilhelm and Birigit (1985) : *Dokumente 1967–1985. Fotos, Briefe, Texte,* Frankfurt/Main, 3ff. The Viennese group called themselves the 'Austrian Film-makers' Cooperative' (1968) and referred to themselves as 'Expanded Cinema'. See: Newspaper article: Hajek, Peter., McLuhan, Für. (1968) 'Bazooka Joe und die Garbo' in *Kurier,* March 25 3.
32. Interview with Wilhelm Hein, December 8 2004.
33. Interviews with Marko Babac, February and March 2004.
34. Interviews with Marko Babac, February and March 2004.
35. My translation. Interview with Wilhelm Hein, December 8 2004.
36. My translation, for the original text see: Weibel, Peter. (1972) 'Aktion statt Theater' in *Neues Forum. Österreichische Monatsblätter für kulturelle Freiheit,* Nr. 221/ Mai 48–52, 50.
37. On such claims of avant-garde movements, especially the Expanded Cinema, in detail: Schober, Anna. 'Seduction through destruction: The political potential of aesthetic trick's in Robert Hariman, Ernesto Laclau, Dilip Gaonkar (eds.), (2008) Trope, Affect and Democratic Subjectivity, Chicago, (in print).
38. Interview with Dieter Schrage, former member of the *Freies Kino* in Vienna, February 10 2004.
39. Interviews with Marko Babac, February and March 2004.
40. Richard Dyer points out how entertainment in mass media can embody Utopianism at the level of sensibility. On this see: Dyer, Richard. (1977) 'Entertainment and Utopia' in Simon During (ed.), (1993) *The Cultural Studies Reader,* London and New York, pp. 271–283.
41. According to this shared, Utopian orientation the reference points for both groups are similar too: both refer quite often to the *New American Cinema,* as well as to Dadaism or to the Russian directors of the revolution: Sergej Eisenstein and Dziga Vertov. According to their demarcations and programmes the German and Austrian Expanded Cinema sticks quite strict to this set and extends it mainly to other avant-gardists such as Surrealism. On this see the historical references in: Hein, Michelis, Wiest, XSCREEN, 1971. The Yugoslavia Black Cinema used a more varied set of references. So for instance, especially at the beginning, the influence of Italian Neo-Realism was quite strong, connections to the French *Nouvelle Vague* are frequent and especially often Leni Riefenstahl is mentioned as an example for an aesthetic challenge to totalitarianism. See: Interviews with Marko Babac, February and March 2004. And Interview with Dušan Makavejev, October 4 2007.
42. For example: Interview with Dušan Makavejev, October 4 2007.
43. The use of such a trichotomy instead of the simple dichotomy 'public-private' is advocated by Alan Wolfe. (1997) 'Public and Private in Theory and Practice: Some Implications of an Uncertain Boundary' in Jeff Weintraub and Krishan Kumar (eds.), *Public and Private in Thought and Practice. Perspectives on a Grand Dichotomy,* Chicago and London, 182–203, 196f.
44. With reference to concepts developed by Hannah Arendt, the project does not see the public sphere as a pre-given entity, but as one that is constituted via people's actions, forms of speech and visible and audible interventions as well as by their perceptions and gestures in a multi-vocal and conflictual way. Hannah Arendt, Vita activa oder: Vom tätigen Leben, Munich and Zurich 1998 (1958), especially 71f.
45. On this: Marc Garcelon, (1997), 'The Shadow of the Leviathan: Public and Private in Communist and Post-Communist Society' in Jeff Weintraub and Krishan Kumar (eds.), *Public and Private in Thought*

and Practice. Perspectives on a Grand Dichotomy, Chicago and London, pp. 303–332. And: Wolfe. (1997), *Public and Private in Theory and Practice*, 182ff.

46. The notion of 'informal public sphere' in order to designate the political relevant diversity of state-independent activities and interactions in totalitarian societies was formulated first by Oleg Yanitskii. See: Yanitskii, Oleg. (1993), *Russian Environmentalism: Figures, Facts, Opinions*, Moscow.

47. On this see: Crossley, Nick. (1999), Working Utopias And Social Movements: An Investigation Using Case Study Materials From Radical Mental Health Movements In Britain' in *Sociology*, 33/, pp. 809–830.

48. Pomian, Krzystof. (1990), 'Religion and Politics in a Time of Glasnost' in Ronald J. Hill (ed.), *Restructuring Eastern Europe. Towards a New European Order,* Worcester, pp. 113–129.

49. On this: Garcelon, Marc. (1997), Shadow of the Leviathan, espec, p. 311.

50. Thus, in a manifesto for her action TAPP UND TASTKINO (Touch-Cinema) – when Valie Export wore a small box fitted with a curtain and called the 'cinema' over her otherwise naked breasts and asked people on the street to 'visit' this small box – she claimed: 'The senses will be freed and this process can in no way be integrated into official rules. Because it leads to a direct liberation of sexuality'. My translation, see: VALIE EXPORT, TAPP UND TASTFILM, unpublished manuscript, p. 1.

51. Interview with Karpo Godina, June 18 2007.

52. Scheugel, Hans. (2002), *Erweitertes Kino. Die Wiener Filme der 60er Jahre*, Vienna, p. 142.

53. *Jutro/Morning* (Puriša Dordević, 1967) or *Zaseda/The Ambush* (Živojin Pavlović, 1969) for example represented conflicts between partisans during or immediately after the war.

54. In this representation of 'pure' – non-motivated by any narration and enhanced – conflict and struggle *Plastični Isus* resembles another film *Mlad i Zdrav Kao Ruza/Young and Healthy like a Rose* (Jovan Jovanović, 1971), which was not shown publicly until 2006.

55. Novaković, Slobodan. (1969), 'Naša decenija: 1960 – 1969/ Ili: Teze za razgovor o jugoslovenskom filmu danas' in Filmska Kultura, 7, XII, pp. 42–50. On the official reactions on this: Interview with Duško Dimitrovski, September 24 2007.

56. Interview with Dušan Makavejev, October 4 2007.

57. Interviews with Marko Babac, February and March 2004.

58. My translation; for the original text see: Weibel, Peter. (1973), *Kritik der Kunst. Kunst der Kritik*, Munich, p. 62.

59. Interview with Birigit Hein, December 4 2004, and interview with Wilhelm Hein, December 8 2004.

60. By representing the usually non-legitimate gazing onto dead bodies here, similar as in pornographic photography, a knowledge is staged, consisting in being let in on having an idea of what the illegitimate or the repressed looks like. On this dimension of pornographic photography: Solomon-Godeau, Abigail. (1991), 'Reconsidering Erotic Photography: Notes for a Project of Historical Salvage' in *Photography at the Dock: Essays on Photographic History, Institutions, and Practices,* Minneapolis, pp. 220–237, 230.

61. For example: Palm, Michael. (1996), 'Which way? Drei Pfade durchs Bild-Gebüsch von Kurt Kren' in Hans Scheugel (ed.), *Ex Underground. Kurt Kren. seine Filme*, Vienna, pp. 114–129, 124.

62. So for example the magazine *Das Argument* demanded that one has to rethink the relation between repression of the sexual drive and anti-Semitic persecution complex, on the one hand and its execution in manifest cruelness on the other hand. See: Fritz Haug, Wolfgang. (1965), 'Vorbemerkung' D in *Das Argument* Nr. 32, p. 30.

63. On this see: Schober, Anna. (2008), *Ironie, Montage, Verfremdung. Ästhetische Taktiken und die politische Gestalt der Demokratie*, Vienna (forthcoming).

64. Interview with Dušan Makavejev, October 4 2007.

65. Interview with Karpo Godina, June 18 2007. And: Interviews with Marko Babac, February and March 2004.

66. Fleck, Robert. (2003), *Die Mühl-Kommune. Freie Sexualität und Aktionismus. Geschichte eines Experiments*, Köln, 63ff.

67. See, for example, the catalogue of an exhibition she made in Vienna in 1975: VALIE EXPORT. (1975) Magna. *Feminismus: Kunst und Kreativität*, exhibition catalogue, Vienna (reprint).

68. Weibel, Peter. (2006), *DasOffene Werk, 1964–1979*, Ostfildern , 876f.

69. Interview with Birigit Hein, December 4 2004 and interview with Wilhelm Hein, December 8 2004.

5

PUBLIC SPACE: THE CITY IN ARMENIAN LITERATURE

Vardan Jaloyan

It is still possible to see young people in Yerevan who gather together somewhere and do nothing. From time to time they are being approached by other young people. Those who have things to do, or those who are simply bored and tired of doing nothing, leave. In working-class districts they physically squat, providing food for jokes to the critics of Armenian kitsch – *rabiz*.[1] I should mention that this critique is shared during similarly purposeless (but critical) get-togethers. When it becomes late, someone offers to disperse, or this happens without words. Of course, they come together to communicate, but often this communication is minimal: they converse with their mere presence. So, their message is limited to forming a composition with their bodies, in this case a *krug*.

This is an example of an open group which one can join and leave voluntarily. There are minimal rules that have to be obeyed; for example it is prohibited to spit in the *krug*. The place of get-togethers is not accidental but can be easily relocated. The definiteness of the place, the aimlessness and at the same time convenience of get-togethers point to the aesthetic aspect of the phenomenon. Certainly, this phenomenon is not unique to Yerevan but there is a peculiarity worth mentioning: from time to time one of the adults, or a few of them, mainly similarly bored retired elders, for some reason, or without any reason at all, try to disperse those groups. Often they get annoyed by the aimlessness of these gatherings. Adults or elders often feel that parental control is lacking from these groups.

Such purposeless gatherings can be found amongst the employees of non-productive or even productive sectors in the late Soviet years. The Soviet government had promised that by 1980 we would achieve communism in our country. In a sense, millions of people who were busy with vain conversations during their working hours, achieved this promise since communism also emerges from a utopia of a civil society that excludes control.

The above-mentioned allows us to claim that in the 1960s, through the 1980s, there was an ongoing process of weakening central control and making the Soviet system public. This culminated in the late 1980s and early 1990s with the collapse of the Soviet Union. This process evolved through spatial expansion; extending from kitchens to other closed spaces such as academic and educational institutions, and later to open places such as cafes, parks and other public and recreational zones. A few cafes were especially significant: Skvaznyachok, Poplavok and Kazerog. The most superfluous strata of the Soviet society – the intelligentsia used to meet in these places and discuss issues of public and social relevance. I call this the most superfluous strata since the Communist Party was not only the people's consciousness but also its mind: for a humanities scholar there was nothing left to do or to think about.

Control has a temporal dimension: its arrows are directed towards a goal or an aim, while its opposite, the lack of control releases the being from the distortions of time, liberating from the gaze the spatial structure of our inhabitation – the city.

By looking at the historical conception of the city, we can claim that it is a compilation of an imaginary project – a paradise or utopia and a real, natural topos. With the emergence of the city, the human being stepped into a new phase of being which would seem paradoxical and fantastic at the same time. On the one hand, it was connected with the search for an earthly paradise, on the other hand, with insecurity, moral decline and decay, suffering and labour. This duality is revealed in the mythologies of upper Jerusalem as virgin-city and the Whore of Babylon in the vivid descriptions of John's *Revelations*.

On the highway leading to Yerevan, one can see billboards of public advertizing depicting the panorama of the city and a child with his finger in his mouth in the foreground. The billboard is to illustrate the attachment of a Yerevani to his/her city. The message 'I love my city' implies this. As with any kind of symbol, not the reality but something that has been lost is signified. We will try to read the image to comprehend the meaning of the 'city'.

Donald Woods Winnicott was one of those psychologists who elaborated on the phenomenon of finger-sucking by children. If the child is unable to cope with the mother's temporary absence, it anticipates the mother by sucking its own finger. If it can cope with this absence, it will then hum or put its whole fist or the edge of the blanket in its mouth. Winnicott called these objects and phenomena 'transitional objects and phenomena'.[2] The above- mentioned billboard indicates that the city is a transitional object. But what do I mean by this?

Talking about the child's ability to comprehend or inter-comprehend the reality, Winnicott explores the available illusion to the child which becomes an inseparable part of art and religion when the child becomes an adult. In his 'Transitional Objects and Transitional Phenomena, a Study of the First Not-Me Possession'[3] Winnicott writes that we consider a madman the one who, being an adult, still demands us to accept his/her subjective imagination as the objective reality and to understand his/her fantasies. But when the adult is capable of getting pleasure from his/her transitory personal sphere without posing any demands, then we are able to accept his/her existence, to respect his/her imaginary experiences, and if we wish, to get together in a group and share our imaginary experiences. This is a common way of creating groups. Examples of such groups are the Association of Art Critics that arguably constitutes a public sphere, the rabiz krug and etc.

At times, the city as a transitory object is governed by the unreal, which results in the identification of the city with madness. We can recall Dostoevsky's Petersburg which is extremely unreal and alien to a Russian and incapable of providing the continuity of his/her human experiences and ensuring the possibility of living together. As Masud Khan mentions in his article on Winnicott, the concept of transitory object has its equivalent in literature and art. Bringing together the real and the imaginary, art creates a new reality and new unity.[4]

In order to understand literature we should approach the text doubly: on the one hand in order to get pleasure from reading, on the other hand we should attribute realness to events and personages without forgetting that they are fictitious.

Armenian symbolist poet Vahan Terian created the symbol Erkir Nairi.[5] Nairi is the name of a part of the Armenian Highland mentioned in Assyrian inscriptions. This symbol is born in an inner reality. It is not pre-determined, and as a phenomenon of an inner reality, it discovers its own boundlessness and vastness. Erkir Nairi is also a name of a new unity, and the author clarifies the principles of this unity in his articles 'Spiritual Armenia'.[6] It is important that he contrasts the spiritual Armenia with the ideal of the state – the police Armenia. When the article was written, Armenia was not yet independent but people had certain expectations. Hence, if we locate the 'transitional space' between the material-productive-economic and the official-ritualistic-phantasmic spheres, then with Terian, who was once described as a mystic-anarchist, Armenia is not so much a cultural sphere but a spiritual one which absorbs the official through transcending the material sphere.

In 1915 Armenia faced the Genocide. A few years later it became independent, then soon after was Sovietized. Following these events, another Armenian poet Eghishe Charents wrote the novel Erkir Nairi. The first part of the novel is wholly dedicated to the description of public spaces and public personae in the city of Kars, as well as to the presentation of the early twentieth century Armenian public sphere – tea houses, clubs and etc; as if the author seeks to find out the reasons for the tragedies of his country and his hero within the public sphere. Where is Erkir Nairi located? Perhaps in the virtual reality of the nationalist party Dashnakcutyun[7] woven with all the rules of the world wide web

It weaves and weaves its web – with steel and iron weaves it from city to city, country to country. But it is not visible: it is inevitable and intangible as a miracle. It is an incomprehensible miracle: a horrifying secret, an amazing amazement.[8]

The stream of consciousness of the hero of the novel, Mazuti Hamo, whose character is certainly influenced by Andrei Beli's *Petersburg*, is described as an inner reality, his illusory experience (if we borrow from Winnicott), a type of madness which culminates in a collapse – a suicide. Or, as Charents himself describes it in the introduction of the novel: 'Perhaps it is true that *Erkir Nairi* is a mirage: a fiction, myth, brain agony, heart ache...No more *Erkir Nairi*, but only people who inhabit the corner of the world called Armenia, which has now become a Soviet Socialist Republic.'[9]

The sign *Erkir Nairi* is replaced with the sign Soviet Armenia, as if the poet-novelist is trying to transfer the object of his hero's inner reality to outer reality. It seems that the Bolshevik poet shares the Marxist critique of the public sphere and civil society: the in-between, 'transit' space does not exist; it is either subject to the control of the superstructure as with Mazuti Hamo or that of the private commercial sector.

In the Armenian literature of the first half of the twentieth century, we can find other descriptions of pre-revolutionary urban life: Vahan Totovents' *Life on the Old Roman Road* (1933),[10] Axel Bakunts' *Kyures* (1935)[11] and Gourgen Mahari's *Burning Gardens* (1966).[12] All these, together with Charents, are constituent parts of the same project that belong to the same generation of writers.

With Stalin's dictatorship, the public sphere disappeared, and with it disappeared the literary genre that mapped the city space in that now the dialectic evolved only within time. The genre reappears again in the 1990s. However, a qualification should be made: since we are talking about the practices of mapping, this particular practice of mapping the city space in literature is marginal in relation to other dominant practices, and particularly, to the nationalist one which tells the story about historical Armenia and the outcome of the Karabagh conflict. When I contrast these two practices of mapping, I imply also the difference between national and civil society as two different experiences of spatial collectivity. Those writers who were trying to resist the marriage of social-nationalism and Socialist Realism, were getting their inspiration from the street. The immense popularity of the urban bard songs of Rueben Hakhverdzian from the early to mid 1990s are evidence of the above-mentioned. The absence of this genre in the last decade is also indicative.

One of the crucial works about the city in this period is the poem *City* by Violette Grigoryan.[13] This long poem, provides a panoramic view of the Yerevan of the 1990s. It starts with the description of a provincial girl's arrival to the city and her temptation with the city life. The poem ends with her fall: she is raped several times. These events are imaginary rather than real; as if they are phantasms that construct the subject. The poem which appears between a subjective phantasm and reality is a space of writing that coincides with the public sphere. For a young woman who came to Yerevan, there are numerous dangers that prevent her from moving freely in the social landscape. Everywhere the danger of violence persists, but the most essential are the national moral taboos.

The public sphere can only be formed by autonomous subjects, which means that they should put aside moral principles for the sake of communication. That is why the mythologem of the bourgeois city is the whore-city. In the inferno of the bourgeois city, the poet is not accompanied by Virgil but by a whore. By describing the whore-city, the poem opposes its architectonics to the architectonics of poetry which is equivalent to the architectonics of the ideal city. The city ends with the author's urge to her poem to be patient. Nevertheless, the autonomous subject who is not fully formed, witnesses the failure to form a public sphere. The important feature of this poem is that the city is identified with the poem itself. One can assume that this is possible since both belong to the category of 'transitional phenomena'.

One can recall Ashot Khachatryan's poem *Daughter of a Bitch* compiled as a series of quotations from Henry Miller. The title is taken from Miller's *Tropic of Cancer*,[14] only that Paris is replaced with Yerevan, and the Milleresque hypo-maniacal excitement with melancholic disappointment.

In all of these cases, literature maps an imaginary landscape, a place of encounter with asocial, immoral marginals turned into autonomous subjects who create their own collective , which is the literary bohemia. It is the imaginary city of the bohemia that they project onto the actual city plan. Perhaps there are parallels here with the Baudelairian *flâneur*.

Baudelaire was translated into Armenian in the beginning of the last century and then again in the 1970s. The span between these two periods is arguably the time of absence for the public sphere, and hence, the parallels are not accidental. What brings together Baudelaire and the authors I have mentioned, is the genius of melancholy which makes the poet search for something he has never lost.

Tigran Paskevichyan starts his *Bitter Stikh*[15] with the following verse:

> I looked for you, Yerevan
> In crazy minds
> In the eyes of pregnant women
> At the feet of the drunk.[16]

And concludes:

> And in my solitary grievance
> And in my repetitive verses-
> As it has never been determined,
> I never found you, Yerevan.

Following Walter Benjamin, we can state that we are not dealing with a national art but with the allegorical alienated gaze.[17] Nevertheless, there is an essential difference between the hero who wanders as a Baudelairian *flâneur* and the nationalist-patriotic one. If the above-mentioned authors' heroes wander in order to assert the existing differences within the social space, and the pleasure of wandering is exactly in finding these differences, the nationalist writer, by wandering through the landscape of his country, strives to assert a specific national *self-sameness*.

Yerevan's *flâneur* formed in the early 1970s, when in the shade of the centrally planned state economy, traces of market economy were emerging with underground businesses. Following Benjamin's analyses, *flâneur* drives the intelligentsia into the market not merely to observe the *flâneur* but to find a consumer, a buyer of its product. The bohemia emerges exactly in the state of inbetweenness when the intelligentsia still has maecenats but also begins to realize itself in the market. The undecidedness of its economic situation corresponds to the undecidedness of its political position.[18]

It should be stated that perhaps this parallel with underground commerce makes him both a bohemian and locates him in the underground since this is where he has to find his clientele. This is not dissidence since his undecided economy relates to his similarly undecided political views. Bohemia is a locus of the decay of social roles and rituals, that which marginalizes its members and makes them fight on the side of anti-social forces. City is a transitional object that fuses together the images of the city as both a real and dead woman which will disappear with the disappearance of the state machine and market aggression.

In Soviet Armenia as well as in the Soviet Union in general, American jeans were a symbol of this underground commerce. Rarely original and often self-made somewhere between Odessa and Ashtarak, they were the most profitable product of underground commerce. This self-madedness was also characteristic of the Soviet Armenian bohemia, and especially of its Soviet modernist art. Jeans are a product of mass consumption which underlines the loss of quality. When they are worn-out, they signify the degree of emancipation from social qualities and values. In the Soviet Union they pointed to the social *super-quality*, the belonging of their wearer to the nomenclature of aristocratic intelligentsia. This is where the difference between the mass character of 'authentic' jeans and their Soviet self-made equivalents reside.

The most significant work for my analyses is Vahram Martirosyan's relatively recent novel *Landslide* of 2000.[19] The novel describes a landslide in the city: the buildings are sinking underground which can be considered as a symbol of Yerevan's capitalist re-construction. Public spaces, public habits and phenomena are conveyed through the hero's daytime wanderings. It is an important factor that the hero, or more precisely, the anti-hero, has an obsessive character which stresses the tension between the return and non-return. The Benjaminian alienated allegorical gaze comes to being through the anonymous negative hero. In the case of a positive hero, the danger of identification would be greater.

This brings the novel closer to Baudelaire's project: *The Flowers of Evil* were also intended to direct the alienated gaze to the panorama of Paris under construction. The panorama, as Benjamin has shown, is inseparable from the capitalist reconstruction of the city: a reconstruction capable of creating only one thing – a landslide.[20] The poet is the only one who is able to preserve its transient and decaying outlines.

The novel encompasses elements of anti-utopia, Menippean satire and popular literature. The plot is divided into two sections: 'the upper' and 'lower' parts. Having in mind the theory of 'constructing imaginary communities' through transitional phenomena, we can state that the post-socialist capitalist formation, the 'upper' collectivity, is absorbed within the symbolic organ put together by the mass media and epitomized in the newspaper *Fast*. The 'lower' collectivity, being a space for poverty and police violence, fails to symbolize this unique 'real' in the public space: the hero refuses to give a press-conference after being threatened by the police, the only written documentation disappears, etc. In fact, the 'lower' exists only because of brutal fantasies that appear in old women's tales. An old lady tells the hero and his girlfriend about 'the lower' part in the form of folk fairy tales. It seems that in Martirosyan's Yerevan, all the constellations of segmented traditionalism from traditional toasts to funerals are at play. Along with these, there are also some new stereotypes – normative dialogues from English textbooks, advertizings and etc. Even traditional old stereotypes are contaminated by the virus of fetishistic consumption. It is as if what seems to be permanent, for example, the custom, exists only as a product for trade. Charity and the public sphere are similarly products, like the NGO Pity the 38 Children established by the hero of the novel. Again we have to refer to Benjamin's concept of ambiguity and fetishism. The first is a frozen moment of the dialectic, a Utopia, while the dialectic image reflects a dream-like world. Such an image reflects the product as such: as a fetish.[21]

The second part of *Landslide* starts with the meeting of the hero with a young woman on Barbeque Avenue. Because of a landslide they find themselves underground, in a kind of hell where they are persecuted. The woman's figure appears in the background of an unreal ritualistic-mechanical life: the spectre of communism, an illegitimate offspring of authorial humanism, an idea of transcendence for literature-lovers. The life conveyed is so unreal that it disappears in the cellars of the police station. Nevertheless, what Martirosyan propagates is the 'treasure' of the public sphere, a hidden 'resource', a location of a Utopia, a project of a future public space.

Talking about the art of memory and the theory of common places, Svetlana Boym writes that memory is born after a disaster. She refers to the Greek legend of Scopas and Simonides of Ceos where the latter was asked to identify all the victims who died under the ruins of Scopas' house. He could recall each and every one of them by remembering their sitting locations. The place itself gets connected to the name of the dead, and Simonides realizes that the art of memory, so crucial for poets, needs to be trained by memorizing verses and people through locating them in familiar places. The art of memory was born on the ruins of Scopas' house.[22]

In Armenia the art of memory was 'born' after the disaster of 1915, and revived the second time on the ruins of the Soviet Union. In both cases it appeared briefly in order to disappear again and pave the way for new times – the times of oblivion: the first time we were forced to forget our national identity during Stalin's regime and the second time we are made to forget the criminal origins of today's Scopas' wealth.

Vardan Jaloyan is a literary and cultural critic in Yerevan, Armenia.

Notes

1. *Rabiz* is an abbreviation of Russian *rabochee iskusstvo* – the art of the working class, which, in the Armenian slang, means mass culture, an equivalent of the Yugoslav *turbofolk*.
2. Winnicott, D. W. (1953) 'Transitional Objects and Transitional Phenomena, a Study of the First Not-Me Possession', *International Journal of Psycho-Analysis,* 34 pp. 89–97.
3. Ibid.
4. M. Masud R. Khan and D. Winnicott (1986) *Holding and Interpretation: Fragment of An Analysis,* London: Karnac Books.
5. *Erkir* literary means 'country' in Armenia. However, it implies a kind of *Sensucht* for the lost home (by A.H.).
6. Terian, Vahan. (1989) *Erkeri Joghovatsu,* Yerevan pp. 335–350 (in Armenian).
7. *Hay Heghapokhakan Dashnakcutyun* (Armenian Revolutionary Federation) was one of the first Armenian political parties established in 1890. They were the governing party during Armenia's two years of independence from 1918–1921 (by A.H).
8. Charents, Egishe. (1987) *Erkeri Joghovatsu.* Yerevan: Sovetakan Grogh, vol. 4, p. 79 (trans. A.H.) (in Arm.).
9. Ibid., p. 10.
10. Totovents, Vahan. (1933)*Kyanqy Hin Hromeakan Chanaparhi Vra.* Yerevan: Yerevan Pethrat Press.
11. Bakunts, Axel. (1933) *Kyures.* Yerevan: Yerevan Pethrat Press,(in Arm.).
12. Mahari, Gourgen. (1963) *Ayrvogh Aygestanner.* Yerevan: Hayastan Press.
13. Grigoryan, Violette. (1997) 'The City', in *Horizon* Literary edition, n. 10, p. 158.
14. Miller, Henry. (1963) *Tropic of Cancer.* London: Calder.
15. *Stikh* is the Russian word for poem. It is used in the Armenian slang. (A.H.)
16. askevichyan, Tigran. (2001) *A Prayer by Itself.* Yerevan, p. 40.
17. Benjamin, Walter. (1989) *Capitale du XIX siecle: le livre des passages.* Paris : Cerf.
18. Ibid.
19. Martirossyan, Varhram. (2000) *Landslide,* Yerevan.
20. Benjamin, Walter. (1989) *Capitale du XIX siecle: le livre des passages.* Paris : Cerf..
21. Benjamin, Walter. (1989) 'N [re the theory of knowledge, theory of progress]', in Gary Smith ed., *Thinking Through Benjamin.* University of Chicago Press, pp. 43–83.
22. Boym, Svetlana, *Common Places: Mythologies of Everyday Life in Russia,* Cambridge, MA: Harvard University Press, 1994.

6

YOU TELL ME: A TOPOGRAPHY

Jane Rendell

This chapter is a topography which emerges through my engagement with the work of four artists – Jananne Al-Ani, Tracey Moffatt, Adriana Varejão, and Richard Wentworth – exhibited for (hi)story, Kunsthalle, Thun (2005). The works invite me in; they draw me close to tell me stories of places. Some I enter through my imagination, others by remembering, travelling back to my childhood in the Middle East. These are journeys to places both external and internal, they take me outside myself and offer me new geographies, new possibilities, but they also return me, altered, to myself, to my own biography, my own interior. This writing is a back and forth movement, a travelogue which takes place across inside and outside, across the sites of engagement between critic and work.

* * *

They tell each other stories, back and forth, from behind their hands, the words slip like cherries, full and glossy. They pass them from one to another.

Along the horizon he paces, back and forth, a tiny figure, smoking.

As a child, my movements followed the pattern of my father's work: Dubai, El Fasher, Kabul, Mekele. At the age of eleven, I was told I was coming back to England with my mother and sister. 'Coming back'; the phrase implied I was returning to a place I had already been. But I had never lived in England before; England might have been my parents' home, but it was not mine.[1]

They speak of an absent man.

Jananne Al-Ani, *Echo, The Visit* (2004).

Jananne Al-Ani, *Muse, The Visit* (2004).

The Visit (2004). A work in two parts: Production stills from *Muse* (2004) 16mm film, transferred to DVD, 15 min. single channel projection. 190 x 300 cm. Photographs: Effie Paleologou. Stills from *Echo* (1994–2004) VHS transferred to DVD, 10 min. four channel projection. 30 x 30 cm each. Commissioned by Film and Video Umbrella and Norwich Gallery. *Courtesy of the artist.*

A tiny figure, smoking, on the dry crust of the earth.

Once the women were back at home, my father continued to traverse the drier areas of the globe. He is a hydro-geologist, a man who looks for water to bring it to the surface. He does this in lands that are not his own, for people whose languages and customs he has to learn anew each time in each place.

Lips part and then come together; words blow in gusts.

On the dry crust of the earth, lacerated with cracks, scarred by the sun.

He is a man with property: land and wives. Inside the walls of his house are sunlit orchards full of dark purple fruit; among the trees his wives sit. Dressed in shades of red, some of the women have covered their faces, others have painted their toe nails pink. From a distance, these women watch us arrive, disappearing inside as the foreigners draw closer. The guests are taken upstairs to an empty veranda overlooking the garden. The only furniture here is a carpet laid out in a long line down the middle of the room. Men sit cross-legged in turbans around the edge of the carpet and eat from the dishes laid out in front of them. We are the only women: my mother, my sister and myself.

Hands flicker. The patterns they gesture echo the flutter of speech.

Scarred by the sun, as the day shortens, his shadow grows longer.

After the meal, as we walk through the dark house to leave, I see a pair of eyes watching me from behind a screen. The eyes belong to a girl whose hands glint with silver. This is his youngest wife, once a nomad, who carries her wealth in the jewels on her fingers. Or so you tell me.

When you look at me, you see only a curtain of black obscuring my face.

She tells me she taught the sheik's sister's daughter English, and because of this she was allowed to enter the harem. She saw that beneath their abbas, the women wore make-up. When, for her labours, she was offered a gift, she asked for a black abba with a gold trim and a gold leaf burqua, the costume that only the wives of the sheik were permitted to wear.

You watch me drag my brush through the knotted strands again and again.

She was born on the eve of the haj. For her entrance, and her mother's labour, her mother received a second gift. This time, the sheik also sent his apologies. 'Sorry', he said, 'so sorry. For a boy I would have sent a watch, but for the girl – a gold coffee pot on a gold chain.'

You can't see me, but from behind the veil of my hair, I can see you.

As a hajia I will never have to make the journey to Mecca. Or so she tells me.

*

Jananne Al-Ani, *Untitled* (2002). Production still from *Untitled* (2002), DVCam transferred to DVD, 3 min. single channel projection. Dimensions variable. Commissioned by Terra Incognita. *Courtesy the artist.*

I can see a man in the distance on the horizon. He approaches me to ask if he might be the odd man out. 'Why', I ask, 'do you think you are the odd man out, is it because you are only one man among so many women?' 'No', he says, 'I think it is because I speak without words: objects have their own stories to tell; once found, they can speak for themselves.'

'You are not the odd man out', I tell him, 'two of these women also tell stories without words, they tell each other stories through places'.

She tells me her story.

How she served you on her knees; buffed the wooden banister, brushed the stone steps, polished the tiled floor at the bottom of the staircase, until her hands bled.

How you took her brown cheeks between your white hands and ripped at the flesh. In your too-tight crinoline, you held her down, beat her crumpled. You hacked her hair off. Clumps of black silk, slits on the white tiles.

She streamed out, escaped to far away, to the palace of her imaginings. The lilac winds of the laudanum desert blew her upwards. She hovered over ceramic-scapes, plates whose edges just touched, and tiles of blue, white and primrose.

Soon this was all there was to see, endless surfaces smooth and empty: saunas, hospitals, prisons, and mortuaries – inside was outside.

*

You tell me of a room awash with blood; tiles meet, red seeps; vividness floats, water dilutes.

I tell you of a hot tent, sweating, with sultry breath and a swollen tongue I gush headlong into red. Round and round, down and down, I am pulled into a world beneath the sand. And towards me, staggering out of the redness comes a soldier.

You tell me of a room pristine square, threatened with ragged tears. The walls run thick with flesh, squeezing through incisions sliced into the tile-work. The slits are dark, alive to touch and fit to burst, lined with grease, from torn limbs laced with fat.

I tell you of a floor of polished marble, black, interwoven with white veins, of how I anxiously trace the tiny cracks around the edge for intruders who might, at any moment, slither through.

You tell me of a ruin where the walls have been turned inside out. Their patterned interiors laid bare to the wind, their edges torn open to expose raw inners

You tell me.

* * *

Tracey Moffatt, *Laudanum* (1998). Tone gravure prints on 250 grammes Arches Cover White 100% acid free rag paper. Series of 19 Images. 30 x 22.5 inches (76 x 57 cm). Edition of 60. (TM 01 16/60). Courtesy of the Victoria Miro Gallery, London. Copyright: The Artist.

Richard Wentworth, *Spread* (1997). Ceramic. 6m diameter. *Courtesy of the Artist and Lisson Gallery, London.*

Adriana Varejão, *The Guest* (2004). Oil on canvas. 70 x 50 cm. (ADV 1330). Courtesy of the Victoria Miro Gallery, London. *Copyright: The Artist.*

In *On Histories and Stories*, writer A. S. Byatt examines her fascination with 'topological fictions', fictions where the term topological means 'both mathematical game-playing, and narratives constructed with spatial rather than with temporal images'.[2] She names certain works by Primo Levi, Italo Calvino and George Perec as the most interesting examples of this kind of writing. For me, these authors have different ways of making topological fictions; while Calvino often uses combination and permutation as strategies for constructing the shape of stories, Levi draws on existing empirical structures, such as the elements, to determine the narrative, and Perec's detailed descriptions of actual places are organized to produce fictional spaces.[3] In discussing his own interest in topological fictions, Calvino refers to a review by Hans Magnus Enzensberger of labyrinthine narratives in the work of Jorge Luis Borges and Robbe Grillet, where Enzensberger describes how, by placing narratives inside one another; these authors make places where it is easy to get lost.[4]

The theme of topological fictions is apparent in the works of Al-Ani, Moffatt, Varejão and Wentworth but in different ways. Wentworth's interest, made evident in *Making Do & Getting By* and *Occasional Geometries* (1975–2005), is in seeking out and paying attention to those inanimate objects that already articulate but which have somehow been ignored. In works such as *List (15 months)* (1994) and *Spread* (1997) he positions combinations of things – buckets, plates, spades – in ways that allow them to communicate with one another and 'speak' directly to the viewer.

Varejão also lets matter speak for itself, but in her work, stories are told through spaces not objects. In earlier works such as *Azulejaria Verde em Carne Viva* (2000) and *Parede con Incisão a la Fontana 3* (2002), seemingly endless tiled interiors tell, with their scars and flesh wounds, of repulsion and excess. In later pieces, the disturbances, like the spreading stain of *The Guest* (2004), are subtler, and in works like *O Obsceno* (2004) or *O Obsessivo* (2004) the titles suggest an interest in the recurring relationship between spatial configurations and specific psychic states, particularly those associated with perversion and claustrophobia.

In Moffatt's work there is also an engagement in the emotional qualities of certain types of space; not the internal typologies that intrigue Varejão, but in juxtapositions of inside and outside, explored in *Up in the Sky* (1997) through the dialogue between a remote shack and the desert wilderness. There is also a central spatial motif in *Laudanum* (1998), in this case, a staircase, a metaphor of transition, whose circular form suggests a dynamic tension, allowing connections to be made between upper and lower levels, but also between physical qualities of materials and the altered mental space of drug induced hallucinations, as well as the charged erotic site of the sado-masochistic relationship between the two female characters in the scene caught somewhere between violent physical conflict and an opiated dream.

There is an exploration of the spatial qualities of emotional tension too in Al-Ani's work. *The Visit* (2004), relates *Muse*, where an isolated male figure inhabits a flat desert plane, to *Echo*, a fragmented conversation between female figures, a place where he is referred to, yet absent from. In several other pieces, Al-Ani focuses on spaces that bind and separate individuals: in *Untitled* (2002), a veil of hair brushed by the subject of the image articulates a visual boundary between the viewer and the brushing subject and in *Portraits* (1999) the women who cover their mouths with their hands sever communication between viewing and viewed subjects.

In this increasingly globalized world, the stories many artists and writers have been telling recently concern travel: they tell us where they have come from, where they are going and what it is like along they way. These are stories about lives, yet despite the often powerful autobiographical elements, told as journeys, the narratives take spatial forms: actively referencing special places, generating situated dynamics through various voices, such as I, you and s/he, and inviting the reader or viewer to take up particular yet often ambiguous and changing positions.

My own fascination with topological fictions has focused on what I call 'site-writings'.[5] My interest is in writing spaces rather than writing *about* spaces. In art criticism this approach demands that the critic investigates the position s/he occupies in relation to works, the locations those works refer to and the spatial issues they raise, not only conceptually and ideologically, but also materially and emotionally, in order to produce texts that locate the spatial themes of the art works in written form.

I suggest that the critic always takes up a position, and that this needs to be made explicit through the process of writing criticism. Along with Hal Foster who has examined critical distance in terms of identification,[6] and Isobel Armstrong who has explored the differences between close and distant reading, distinguishing between what she calls a criticism of affect and one of analysis,[7] I would argue that such a project involves rethinking some of the key terms of criticism, specifically judgement, discrimination, and distance. By repositioning the work as a site, 'site-writing' investigates the site of the critic's engagement with a work, adopting and adapting both Howard Caygill's notion of immanent critique where the criteria for making judgements are discovered or invented through the course of criticism,[8] and strategic critique where the critic may make a discriminate judgement at a moment of externality where the work 'exceeds itself' and 'abuts on experience',[9] as well as Mieke Bal's exploration of 'art-writing'.[10] Rather than write *about* the work, I am interested in how the critic constructs his or her writing in relation *to* and in dialogue *with* the work. The focus on the preposition here allows a direct connection to be made between the positional *and* the relational.[11]

Theoretical explorations in literary criticism of the different subject positions authors can occupy in relation to the text, multiple 'I's',[12] for example, as well as 'you' and 's/he',[13] are relevant here, as are the writings of postcolonial critics who have woven the autobiographical into the critical in their texts, combining poetic practice with theoretical analysis to articulate hybrid voices.[14] Critical 'voices' can be objective *and* subjective, distant *and* intimate. From the close-up to the glance, from the caress to the accidental brush, criticism can draw on spaces as they are remembered, dreamed and imagined, as well as observed, in order to take into account the critic's position in relation to a work and challenge criticism as a form of knowledge with a singular and static point of view located in the here and now.

In visual and spatial culture, feminists have drawn extensively on psychoanalytic theory to think through relationships between the spatial politics of internal psychical figures and external cultural geographies.[15] The field of psychoanalysis explores these various thresholds and boundaries between private and public, inner and outer, subject and object, personal and social in terms of a complex understanding of the relationship between 'internal' and 'external' space. Cultural geographer Steve Pile has described it like this:

> While inner life is distinct, there is continuous exchange between the internal and external, but this 'dialectic' is itself interacting with the transactions between 'introjection' and 'projection'.[16]

The psychic processes of introjection and projection, as well as identification, provide a rich source of conceptual tools for exploring the complex relationships made between subjects and others, and between people, objects and spaces. Psychoanalyst Jessica Benjamin has suggested that once we start to think in terms of relationships between subjects, or subjectivity, we have no choice but to consider these intraphysic mechanisms of relation, most importantly identifications: 'Once subjectivity is embraced', she says, 'we have entered into a realm of knowledge based on identifications, hence knowing that is intrapsychically filtered.'[17]

If criticism can be defined by the purpose of providing a commentary on a cultural work – art, literature, film and architecture – then criticism always has an 'other' in mind. The central task of criticism might then be considered as: how does one make a relationship with an 'other'? It is this question that is at the heart of psychoanalytic theory and practice. As Benjamin writes:

> An intersubjective theory of the self is one that poses the question of how and whether the self can actually achieve a relationship to an outside other without, through identification, assimilating or being assimilated by it.[18]

This question – of how it is possible to achieve a relationship with an 'other' – has also been taken up as a pressing enquiry in feminist philosophy. Judith Butler, through discussions of both G. W. F. Hegel's account of the master-slave dialectic and Emmanuel Levinas' exploration of the face of the other, has drawn attention to the ethical aspects of relationships with the 'other'.[19]

> For if I am confounded by you, then you are already of me, and I am nowhere without you. I cannot muster the 'we' except by finding the way in which I am tied to 'you' by trying to translate but finding that my own language must break up and yield if I am to know you. You are what I gain through this disorientation and loss. This is how the human comes into being, again and again, as that which we have yet to know.[20]

Butler points to the work of the Italian feminist philosopher, Adriana Cavarero, who argues that we are exposed to the other from the start, and it is this exposure, which is the condition for political and social life. Cavarero states:

> Autobiography does not properly respond to the question 'who am I?' Rather, it is the biographical tale of my story, told by another, which responds to this question.[21]

Cavarero proposes that our desire to have our life story narrated by another, demonstrates the role of a pre-existing 'other' as foundational to the formation of the subject. Butler suggests that Cavarero turns around the usual progression from the early dyad to social relations, and instead 'ground[s] the social in the dyadic encounter'.[22] Literary critic Mary Jacobus has described 'the scene of reading' in terms of a relation, perhaps a correspondence, which exists between the inner world of the reader and the world contained in the book.[23] Taking up this insightful observation, I suggest that criticism involves such a double movement back and forth between inside and outside. The critic is expected to remain 'objective' or exterior to the work and at the same time he or she is invited inside – to enter the world of the work; the work is physically positioned outside the critic, yet at the same time it may occupy the site of the critic's psychic life igniting interior emotions and memories. This pair of two-way movements between critic and work suspends what we might call judgement or discrimination in criticism, and instead, through what I call the practice of 'site-writing', traces and constructs a series of interlocking sites that relate and locate, that position the 'dyadic encounter' between critic and work.

* * *

These Red Words have been read in parts, read then left, left then read. Objects slipped in between the pages mark the pauses. How long will it be, I ask, before you open a page and tell me another story?

You tell me.

Jane Rendell is Professor of Architecture and Art and Director of Research at the Bartlett School of Architecture, University College London.

Notes

1. The texts in italics have been taken from Rendell, Jane. (2002), 'Travelling the Distance/Encountering the Other', in David Blamey (ed.) *Here, There, Elsewhere: Dialogues on Location and Mobility.* London, Open Editions, pp. 43–54 and Rendell, Jane. (2003), 'To Miss the Desert', in Gavin Wade (ed.), *Nathan Coley: Black Tent.* Portsmouth, pp. 34–43. Both these essays were reworked for Rendell, Jane. (2006), 'An Embellishment: Purdah', in *Spatial Imagination.* London, The Domo Baal Gallery with an associated catalogue essay in Peg Rawes and Jane Rendell (eds) (2005), *Spatial Imagination*, London, The Bartlett School of Architecture, UCL, pp. 34–5. See www.spatialimagination.org.uk.
2. Byatt, A S. (2001), *On Histories and Stories.* London: Vintage, pp. 139–141.
3. See for example, Levi, Primo. (2000), *The Periodic Table.* London: Penguin Books; Calvino, Italo. (1998) *If on a Winter's Night a Traveller.* London: Vintage Classics, and Georges Perec, (1992), *Life: A User's Manual,* London: Collins Harvell.
4. Enzensberger, Hans Magnus. (1996), 'Topological Structures in Modern Literature', *Sur,* (May–June 1966) referred to by Calvino in Italo Calvino (1997), *The Literature Machine.* London: Vintage, p. 25.
5. For an account of the conceptual framework that underpins my practice of 'site-writing' and relates it to the work of other theorists and critics see Rendell, Jane. (2005), 'Architecture-Writing', in Jane

Rendell (ed.) 'Critical Architecture', special issue of *The Journal of Architecture*, v. 10. n. 3, June, pp. 255–64. For a discussion of two pieces of 'site-writing', which transformed over several sites, see Rendell, Jane. (2005) 'Site-Writing', in Sharon Kivland, Jaspar Joseph-Lester and Emma Cocker (eds) *Transmission: Speaking and Listening*, v. 4, Sheffield Hallam University and Site Galler, pp. 169–176 and Jane, Rendell. (2007)'Site–Writing: Enigma and Embellishment', in Jane Rendell, Jonathan Hill, Murray Fraser and Mark Dorrian (eds) *Critical Architecture*, London: Routledge, forthcoming. See also 'Site-Writing: she is walking about in a town which she does not know', Mcfadden, Lesley and Barrac, Matthew (eds) (2007) *Connected Spaces*, special issue of *Home Cultures* forthcoming and 'Curating, Editing, Writing: Critical Spatial Practice', Rugg, Judith (ed) (2007) *Issues in Curating, Contemporary Art and Performance*. Bristol: Intellect Press, forthcoming.

6. See Foster, Hal. (2001) *The Return of the Real: The Avant-Garde at the End of the Century*. Cambridge, Mass.: The MIT Press pp. 223–6.

7. See Armstrong, Isobel. (2000) *The Radical Aesthetic*. Oxford: Blackwell Publishers, p. 87.

8. Caygill, Howard. (1998) *Walter Benjamin: The Colour of Experience*. London: Routledge, p. 34 and p. 79.

9. Caygill, Howard. (1998) *Walter Benjamin: The Colour of Experience*. London: Routledge, p. 64.

10. See Bal, Mieke. (2001) *Louise Bourgeois' Spider: The Architecture of Art-Writing*. London and Chicago: University of Chicago Press, p. xi. See also Norman Bryson, (2001) 'Introduction: Art and Intersubjectivity', Mieke Bal, *Looking in: The Art of Viewing*. Amsterdam: G+B International,) pp. 1–39, p. 12.

11. The significance Trinh T. Minh-ha assigns to the shift from speaking 'about' to speaking 'to' has been stressed by Irit Rogoff who underscores how, instead of taking power relationships to produce spatial locations, it is possible for a change in position to advance a change in relation. See Irit Rogoff's discussion of Trinh T. Minh-ha's assertion in Rogoff, Irit. (1998) 'Studying Visual Culture', Mirzoeff, Nicholas (ed.) *The Visual Culture Reader*. London, Routledge, pp. 14–26, p. 18.

12. Italo Calvino, for example, has explicitly explored the relationship the writer has to his/her writing in terms of position – where a writer stands – inside and/or outside a text. See Calvino, Italo. (1997) 'Literature as Projection of Desire', *The Literature Machine*. London: Vintage, p. 58. In another essay, Calvino discusses the places writers occupy in relation to their writing in terms of their different identities as subjects or 'I's. See Calvino, Italo. (1997) 'Cybernetics and Ghosts', *The Literature Machine*. London: Vintage, p. 15.

13. Roland Barthes has described his choice of authorial voice in terms of four regimes: including an 'I', the pronoun of the self, a 'he', the pronoun of distance and a 'you', a pronoun which can be used in a self-accusatory fashion or to separate the position of the writer from the subject. See Barthes, Roland. (1991) *The Grain of the Voice: Interviews 1962–80*, translated by Linda Coverdale, Berkeley and Los Angeles: University of California Press, pp. 215–6

14. See Anzaldúa, Gloria. [1987] (1999) *Borderlands/La Frontera: the New Mestiza*. San Francisco: Lute Books and Cixous, Hélène. [1975] (1994) 'Sorties', translated by Betsy Wing from Susan Sellers (ed.) *The Hélène Cixous Reader*. London: Routledge.

15. See for example, Friedman, Susan Stanford. (1998) *Mappings: Feminism and the Cultural Geographies Of Encounter*. Princeton, Princeton University Press; Fuss, Diane. (1995) *Identification Paper*. London, Routledge; Grosz, Elizabeth. (1994) *Volatile Bodies: Toward a Corporeal Feminism*. Bloomington and Indianapolis: Indiana University Pres; Rogoff, Irit. (2000) *Terra Infirma*. London: Routledge and Silverman, Kaja. (1996) *The Threshold of the Visible World*. London: Routledge.

16. Pile, Steve. (1999) *The Body and The City*, London: Routledge, p. 91. See also Grosz, *Volatile Bodies*, pp. 27–61.
17. Benjamin, Jessica. (1998) *Shadow of the Other: Intersubjectivity and Gender in Psychoanalysis*, London: Routledge, p. 25.
18. Ibid, p. 80.
19. Butler, Judith. (2001) 'Giving an Account of Oneself', *Diacritics*, Winter, v. 31, n, 4, pp. 22–40.
20. Butler, Judith. (2004) *Precarious Life: The Powers of Mourning and Violence*. London: Verso, p. 49.
21. Cavarero, Adriana. (2000) *Relating Narratives: Storytelling and Selfhood*, [1997] translated by Paul A Kottman, London: Routledge, p. 45.
22. Butler, Judith. (2001) 'Giving an Account of Oneself', *Diacritics*, Winter, v. 31, n, 4, p. 24.
23. Jacobus, Mary. (1999) *Psychoanalysis and the Scene of Reading*. Oxford: Oxford University Press, p. 18.

Richard Wentworth, *The Red Words (Die Roten Worte)* (1997). Aluminium foil, copper, wood and plastics. 41.5 x 53 cm. *Courtesy of the Artist and Lisson Gallery, London.*

Section Three: Identities and Topographies of Everyday Life

7

Routes Through the City: Youth Identities and Spatial Practices in Leipzig

Kathrin Hörschelmann

Introduction

This chapter traces some of the routes of young people in the East German city of Leipzig in order to explore how they perceive, experience and live within transforming urban space. I will ask how their identities are performed in daily spatial practices; how and where they make the city their own; and which aspects of the city help them to forge a sense of belonging at a time of unmooring and deterritorialization. In answering these questions, I aim to keep in mind how forces beyond the reach of individual young people mould the urban landscapes they encounter, while emphasizing that it is only through the performative acts of each young person that these landscapes are 'brought into being' for them.[1] The city as a place of spectacular consumption, for instance, can become a playground for multiple identities, as many studies of youth culture, consumption and urban change have attested.[2] For some it can open a route to exploring and adopting cosmopolitan lifestyles that may or may not be tied to a politics of radical openness and anti-racism.[3] Yet for others, it may produce a sense of lost moorings and disorientation. Both the exclusivity of the city centre as a shoppers' paradise and fears of the presence of 'others' can make it inaccessible to them and have an impact on their routes through the city.

The metaphor of 'routes', rather than roots, is pertinent for describing the embodied spatial and temporal practices through which young people engage urban space. It captures some of that 'shuffling between particular spaces and times' that Amin and Thrift[4] implore us to trace, connecting young people's daily practices to their imagined futures[5] and articulating both the regularity of daily routines and unexpected diversions, whether they are necessitated by changes in the urban landscape, through encounters with others or initiated by individuals. 'Routes' allow us to conceptualize the processes of de- and re-territorialization not as a struggle between fixity and change, between the present and the absent, the macro and the micro, but as a patterned, yet mobile texturing of daily lives, where transformations in urban (and non-urban) landscapes are negotiated through embodied practices and imaginations that are both habitual and necessarily subject to change. Improvization is as much part of these negotiations as the treading of well-used paths. The metaphor of 'routes', thus becomes part of 'another vocabulary, with which to describe the city, one which takes circulation, hybridity and multiplicity as key urban moments, and fixed boundaries as temporary allegiances and alignments'.[6]

Urban change and everyday life

The transformations that have taken place in east and central Europe have entailed significant changes in the ordering and experience of space. For many cities, the peaceful revolutions of 1989 and 1990 heralded a period of contradictory developments and upheavals that symbolized and made material the disorientations experienced in everyday life. Economic decline and rising unemployment, privatization in the housing market coupled with rising rents and house prices, new social inequalities and urban marginalities, derelict infrastructures and declining investments in public ventures went hand in hand with the mushrooming of small enterprizes, new investments into transport infrastructures, growth of the service sector, re-construction of city centres and gentrification in older residential quarters, suburban sprawl, the arrival of new consumer outlets, luxury housing and hotel developments, private leisure facilities, etc.[7] In eastern Germany, these developments combined with a sharp decrease in population due to both falling birth rates and migration to western parts of the unified country.

The city of Leipzig, which is the focus of this chapter, initially lost 80 per cent of its employment in the industrial sector. These losses have been partially recuperated by the slow growth of the service sector, especially media, and recent investments by BMW, Porsche, Amazon and DHL. Yet, unemployment rates are still high, standing at around 18 per cent in 2006. Nearly half the job-less population are long-term unemployed, and 10 per cent of the unemployed are young people between twenty and twenty-five years of age. Social inequalities are beginning to show in the structure of the city and its housing market. Newly gentrified districts such as Leipzig's south west and brand-new suburban housing estates contrast with regenerated, yet depopulated former working class areas and mixed-quality tower-block estates. Public investment has concentrated on developing the transport infrastructure, constructing a new Trade Fair Centre, subsidizing housing renovations and attracting business investments.[8]

Leipzig's urban landscape today continues to display characteristics of the socialist city in some of its built structure, yet new developments in the city centre have focused on eroding this contradictory heritage by removing buildings from the socialist period step by step and replacing them with new shopping centres, banks and hotels. For some, this is an important step towards modernization, while for others, the erosion of a familiar, if troubled heritage is regrettable and not without its own contradictions. Amongst these is the general loss of moorings in a landscape that has been radically overhauled at the same time as social, economic and political changes eroded many of the stabilities of everyday life. The increasing semi-privatization of public space, either directly through property-restitution and the selling of real estate, or indirectly through the introduction of video surveillance and the increasing exclusivity of the centre is another concern for those who saw the peaceful revolution of 1989 as the dawn of a new era of democratic public life, to which public spaces in the city would be central. For a city that became symbolic of the protests against the East German state in 1989, the erosion of the socialist landscape also marks a loss of visible reminders of that past and with them a loss of opportunity for critical reflection.

Youth and post-socialist transformation

In the remainder of this chapter, I will consider how these changes have affected young people's everyday urban rhythms and their sense of place. Young people who grew up after 1989 have, thus far, only been given fleeting attention in the literature on post-socialist urban change. Smith[9] begins to address how urban youth cultures in Leipzig are changing, while Pilkington et al[10] have explored the intersections between local, national and global identities for young people in Moscow and Ul'ianovsk. However, a specific focus on the ways in which young people's spatial practices and cultural identities are mediated through transformations of the city and the extent to which they themselves become part of those transformations has, thus far, received scant attention. Yet, focusing on youth helps us to displace some of the familiar assumptions about past-dependent post-socialist identities, as their experiences with state-socialism are inevitably mediated and may be less important than considering the challenges of growing up at a time of rapid transformations.

For young people in Leipzig the 'exception' of transformation constitutes the norm. They live with and through changes in the city parallel to their own biographical changes which, for those of school leaving age, are dominated by questions of finding further education and work. Young people in Leipzig live their lives in transit in many ways. Depending on their precise age, they may have gone through several changes in the school system, seen their parents get in and out of work, relocated to or within the city, and will often have considered moving to another city, usually in western Germany, for further education and work. The neo-liberal demands of individualization are very much upon them and the pressure to work hard, be flexible and stay mobile is notable in most accounts of school-leaving youths.[11] At the same time, those anchor points which would help to ease some of the difficulties of personal transitions have become weaker as parents may be unable to help financially or with appropriate advice, while meeting places for young people such as clubs and cultural centres have decreased significantly in number, are under-funded and often operate on a short-term basis. The city of Leipzig has sought to compensate for some of this by investing in public sports facilities, but to what extent this is sufficient to provide for different needs and interests is highly doubtful.

Cindi Katz has rightly critiqued the disinvestment in social reproduction that has occurred in sites as diverse as her research locations in urban Harlem and rural Sudan.[12] She clearly draws out the connections between globalization, neo-liberalization and the decline in children's welfare. While Katz emphasizes the creativity and energy with which children tackle the new challenges, she also reminds us of the powerful forces that erode their livelihoods:

> Public responsibility for social reproduction is jettisoned as the workforce is redefined and 'globalized', and responsibility for social reproduction is increasingly relegated to the private realm across disparate geographies at all scales. The strategy has been to abdicate all collective responsibility for reproducing the society as a whole...What kind of geographical imaginations are possible in a population growing up under these conditions? What are the political costs of coming of age in a disintegrating public environment, where the only viable correctives are privately secured?[13]

In thinking about post-socialist urban change and youth identity it is crucial to remember that, even as young people engage creatively and often optimistically with de-territorializing and re-territorializing forces that transform the textures of their everyday lives,[14] they are structurally placed in a subordinate position as they have less independent access to material resources[15] and are denied full citizenship. [16] As such they rarely find their voices listened to in adult policy and planning processes. Families with children are amongst the worst hit by economic recession and the decline in social welfare.[17] Those growing up in poor families bear the greatest burden of change and are forced to adopt a range of livelihood strategies in order to 'domesticate neo-liberalism'.[18] Although I do not explicitly focus on questions of social justice here, it is important to remember the highly uneven conditions which form the background to and are highly influential for young people's engagements with the city.

Materials

The materials I will use in the following sections were produced as part of a larger research project on 'Globalization, cultural practice and youth identities in former East Germany', conducted in Leipzig in 2003.[19] The research involved interviews with fifteen groups of young people, most between the ages of twelve and eighteen. Most of the groups were of mixed gender, though two boy-groups and four girl-groups were also interviewed.[20] Each group worked with me and a research assistant over a period of five weeks, conducting focus group discussions and producing a range of other materials such as diaries, mental maps, photographs and posters. Here, I focus exclusively on the mental maps, photographs and focus group discussions. Participants were given the task of photographing significant places in their everyday life over a period of one week. We discussed these photographs with them the following week and also asked them to draw a mental map on the same theme.

There are several methodological issues to keep in mind when interpreting these materials, some of which are described in a previously published paper.[21] Neither do most of the photographs display everyday life in anything like a strict chronological order, nor are they a complete record of daily spatial practices or always focused on the task. Different understandings of that task lead to different emphases in the photos (e.g. whether important people and objects were shown). Participants brought varying levels of skill to their photography and some made it clear that they had intentionally left out aspects of their everyday lives that they did not want to show. Others also raised questions about the ability of photographs to represent them and what was important to them in a meaningful way. The photo-discussions helped to explain some of these issues and the picture contents, intentions and mistakes, but they clearly left much open to interpretation.

Mental maps introduced another form of representation. They again depended greatly on individual skill, interpretation of the task and degrees of copying within groups. Yet, by being less concentrated on accurate depiction, they were a more open medium for showing the *felt* significance of places and routes through the city and allowed participants to include 'dreamscapes' and 'futurescapes' in their maps. The maps thus worked on a different time-scale than the photographs and allowed participants, depending on ability, to produce more abstract, pre-conceptualized images of their lives. I draw on both these materials here as *traces* rather than as mirrors of 'reality'. They have emerged from young people's lives, but in a mediated, filtered, non-transparent way that is best described as a touching without grasping. As you engage with these images and my interpretation of them, allow them to touch you, while at the same time noticing that much of their significance escapes your grasp.

Routes and routines

In considering young people's attachments to the city, we need to focus not just on spectacular sites or particularly meaningful places, but also on the everyday routines that create *habitual*, embodied relations between person and space. While post-socialist cities are characterized by significant changes in their infrastructure, architecture and function, much of a young person's daily life is taken up by regular *routines* that evolve around institutions such as the school, youth club and family. School takes up most of their time in the day and few young people profess to having a positive attachment to it. Nonetheless, it structures their daily lives in a greater way than any other site, including the regularized routines of getting up in the morning, travelling to school, following its divisions of time and space (lesson/break time, classroom, corridor, school grounds, canteen), finding time for homework, and travelling from school to other sites in the city.

The mental maps and photographs give a good indication of the significance of school for our participants. Not only is it the one site that appears on almost all of their maps and photographs, movement within the city is also frequently shown to be organized around it. School does not necessarily occupy centre-stage on the maps, though. In many cases, participants have drawn it slightly off centre to indicate that it is an important, but not a favourite site. Places such as youth clubs, sports or cultural centres, friends and relations crowd many of the maps and attract far more positive descriptions as aspects of their lives over which they have more control. Nonetheless, they form part of patterned movements through the city, which are connected to social obligations, expectations and responsibilities that make young people's lives far less voluntaristic than is often stereotypically imagined. The density of such sites outside of school and home differs significantly between individual maps, however. For some, time after school is tightly packed and strictly organized around several clubs, extra-curricular courses and visiting

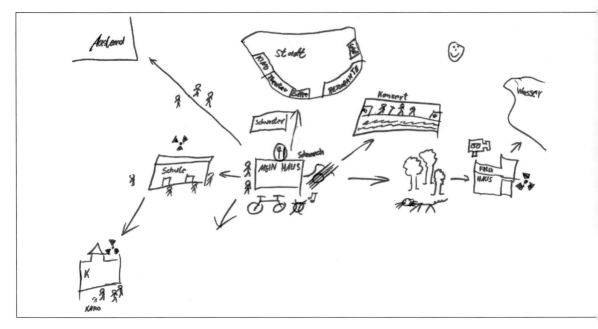

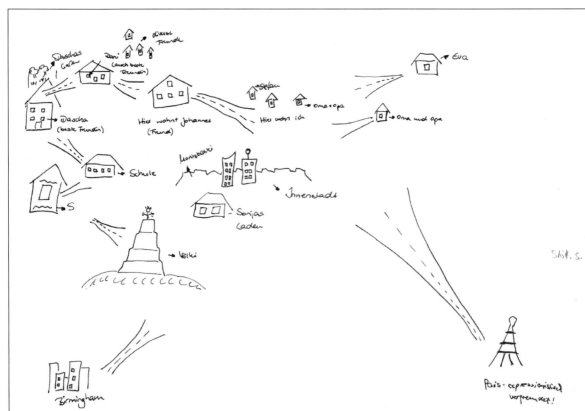

Above and opposite: Mental Maps.

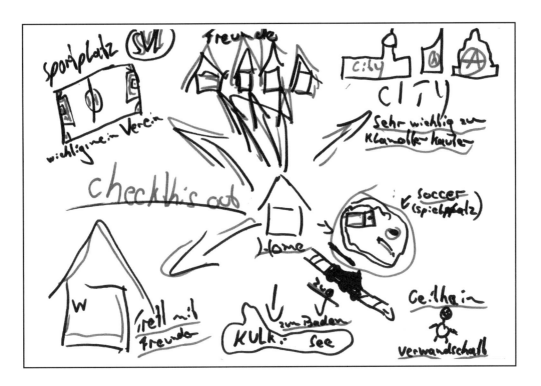

friends and family across the city. For others, it is symbolized by one or two key places such as a youth club or, perhaps, the local shopping centre, a friend's home or a family member's place. There are major differences in the use and extent of leisure activity spaces that relate to the formation of social and cultural capital, as I have argued elsewhere.[22] These differences relate to participant's sociocultural backgrounds, their peer groups, education and parental influences, but they are also part of the process through which a young person's *habitus* is formed,[23] enabling them in differential ways to act within society and to pursue future life options.

The regularized time-spaces through which young people lead most of their daily lives may be situated in specific places, but they transgress the local in many ways, not only because sites such as schools are part of a wider network of institutional structures, but also because the worlds that are lived and imagined through such sites exceed them. It is particularly in schools and clubs that young people encounter some degree of cultural diversity, even if their peer groups are ethnically exclusive, and in lessons or club activities places and times beyond the here-and-now are imagined and sometimes re-enacted. Such activities do not necessarily equate to the promotion or achievement of a 'cosmopolitan ethics,'[24] but they are part of the de-territorialization of 'localities'.

While much of a young person's life evolves around routines beyond her or his control, niches for more independent activity emerge throughout the day in the movement between places and

School.

fixed time-slots. Thus, the journey to school offers opportunities for chatting with friends, listening to music or perhaps just for day-dreaming, people-watching and being alone in the crowd. In Leipzig, school students from an early age tend to make their own way to school by tram, bus or walking. These journeys are not free from adult supervision, but parents rarely accompany them. The journey to and from school occupies much space on the maps and in the photographs. It includes waiting times at the bus- or tram-stops that are valuable periods inbetween, where young people get a moment to themselves. Such 'wasteful' times can be boring, but they can also be a tremendous resource, either just to get a moment to one-self or to spend time with peers. It is at these times that young people make their presence in the city most strongly felt and are often resented for it by fellow adult travellers, especially if they are noisy and less restrained in their behaviour. Waiting times and places are a key dimension of public space for young people, yet one where their presence is most frequently problematized.

Other regular niche-places within their institutionalized daily landscapes include the school grounds and corridors between lessons, playgrounds outside of school (which are a contested terrain between different age groups), shifting meeting places in the city, their own rooms at home, and outdoor spaces such as parks, urban wastelands, open-air swimming pools and, in Leipzig, beaches along the artificial lakes. The latter depend strongly on the seasons and our participants made it clear that their options for meeting friends were highly restricted during the winter as there were fewer places to 'hang-out' without adult interference. Yet, one group had

Spaces in-between: travelling to school.

Niche places: school ground.

found such a place through the help of a parent who had allowed them to convert a loft-room for their own exclusive use. This room had become their main after-school meeting place. For others, youth clubs became the main meeting place during winter.

One of the main changes in Leipzig since 1989 has been the diversification of its retail landscape. The inner city is now dominated by glittering department stores, luxury fashion outlets, hotels, banks, restaurants and, along its fringes, a range of cheaper high-street shops. Participants in our project used these facilities in a highly differentiated way. For some, the inner city offered spectacular multi-cultural experiences and was a site for experimentation with identities, a favourite place for social interactions and the performance of multiple selves. Others rarely ventured into the centre because of its perceived exclusivity and fears about 'stranger-danger' that were particularly connected to the presence of foreigners. For these young people, shopping centres in their neighbourhoods were an alternative site, functioning in much the same way as the city centre, but in an atmosphere that they perceived as safer and less disorientating. Shopping for most participants, but especially for the girls, was an important social activity through which friendships were consolidated and identities negotiated.[25] Rather than locating this beyond the sphere of the public, we need to see shopping centres as somewhere in-between, for while they are certainly controlled and purposefully constructed to facilitate consumption, they continue to be focal points for a wider range of social interactions. More radical critiques

City centre.

of commodity culture not withstanding, what is problematic is the way in which (young) people's actions are regulated within such locations to conform with the imperative to consume and the extent to which they are excluded if they don't. As Jackson cautions:

> ...transforming the public space of the high street into the privatized commercial space of the shopping mall has clear social costs in terms of democratic access and public accountability. While we can exaggerate the democracy and freedom of the city's streets both now and in the past, the domestication of space through purification and privatization necessarily involves increased social exclusion and heightened inequality. How much are we prepared to surrender the control of public space to market forces? How much freedom will be traded for increased security? And who will pay the costs for such perceived benefits in terms of increased surveillance or outright exclusion?[26]

The shopping centre clearly is not 'the street', as much as it may emulate features of it, yet for young people, the street has rarely held the democratic public potential that some urban theorists credit it with.[27] Our critique of the privatization of 'public' space thus needs to be fine-tuned to the specific power-relations that shape access to 'public' space for different groups: 'who and what come to count as being truly 'public' and/or 'political' as well as how and where they can come to count'.[28]

Outdoor space.

For our participants, many of the most important places for social interaction were, in fact, about *disengagement* from adult publics. These places were less about diversity and public engagements than about the claiming of space away from adult supervision, for entertaining relations with peers. The artificial lakes on the fringes of Leipzig offered a superb location for this and were mentioned without fail as a favourite leisure site. Most of the beaches along the lakes are free to access and unsupervized. This makes them ideal for young people on a small budget looking for somewhere to meet their friends outside of the home or a club. It is rare to have such spaces in cities, but the example of Leipzig shows how important they can be to create a sense of belonging to and ownership of the city for young people.

Sense of place

When asked about the places that were most meaningful for them and to which they had the strongest emotional attachments, our participants often misrecognized the spatial orientation of the question and instead mentioned their family relations and friends. Such relations, though perhaps connected to specific sites, travel with people to some extent and are of primary importance for the formation of personal identities. Our participants consequently highlighted them as significant anchor points in their daily lives, even if the relations or friends lived some way away and were only visited during vacation. In addition to significant people, participants also showed great attachments to pets in their photographs. Such images gave an insight into caring aspects of their daily lives, not to mention the enormous significance that pets had in turn for their own sense of wellbeing.

Places invested with particular emotional significance ranged from the urban quarter to far-away, imagined sites of past and future travels. The urban quarter stood out as a significant site for those participants fortunate enough to have close social friendships within their neighbourhood. They highlighted regular face-to-face contacts and the sense of being known and knowing other people as important for their sense of self and place:

> I now live in a street where there are one or two kids per family, so there are lots of kids there, and then everybody knows everybody, but where we lived before, it wasn't like that. Everybody was more anonymous there. There were lots of cars and it was pretty noisy (Ina, 13).

> I used to live in Gholis, well and I liked it better in Gholis then here...In Gholis I could go on the street and see somebody from there and know them, so you could have a chat straight away, so not just people from school...We also had a kind of meeting place, where young people met, but that's disappeared (Tom, 15).[29]

In addition to the urban quarter, the symbolic landscape of Leipzig's inner city figured large in many participants' descriptions of meaningful places, lending them a sense of place beyond the uniformity of some of the newer consumer infrastructures. The two town halls, the church of St Thomas, the university tower, the opera and concert halls, the restored main station and, further out, the monument to the Battle of the Nations, were all mentioned as key sites that made

Urban quarter/neighbourhood.

Leipzig special. Yet, the inner city as a site of consumption and spectacular experience was equally highlighted by many as a major attraction, as it offered opportunities to meet different people and have diverse experiences:

This is the city, that's where I love to go. I could spend all my time there (Laura, 13).

We've just moved and I think it's pretty cool, because it only takes me three minutes to walk to the city centre and there you have all the students, students, students, and the university (Andreas, 16).

Interviewer: Is there something you especially like to do?

Ina: Go to the city centre.

Interviewer: To the city centre. And there?

Ina: To Pimkie.

Interviewer: For shopping?

Ina: Yes, but not to buy anything...

Karo: I like that as well. And I also like to go to the cinema.

The arrival of commodity capitalism in the city was not welcomed by all, however. Seventeen year old Bea, for instance, explained that while typical for Leipzig, she disliked the plush new department store that had come to occupy centre stage on one of the main streets. She was also suspicious of the city's marketing efforts and highlighted instead that the most characteristic feature of Leipzig was its transitory state, symbolized in the many building sites:

Bea: The one thing that I think is typical for Leipzig are the building sites...And I don't like these prestige objects, which Leipzig is advertizing.

Tobi: You have forgotten the main station.

Karl: The main station is nice.

Sven: The main station is the largest dead-end station in Europe. Surely that's typical for Leipzig?

Bea: Yes, but I find that stupid. That's what the council always try to promote, and Leipzig, great, everything is renovated and, I don't know, the new Trade Fair grounds, I find that stupid. It loses all individuality...And here is something else that's typical for Leipzig, my object of hate, although I do go there, but anyway.

I: Why?

Bea: I don't know. I didn't like it right from the start. It looks awful, the building, and I always call it the battle ship of consumer society.

While much of urban planning is concerned with renovating derelict spaces in the post-socialist city, some of our participants argued that it was particularly those sites that gave them a sense of place. Sandra, below, points to the opportunities for hiding that such places offer, thus in turn implying that re-construction elsewhere had taken away places for unsupervized activity:

I also like that despite all the re-construction works, there is still a lot that's authentic, there are still some hiding places, like, it's not completely covered, not completely renovated (Sandra, 18).

What I like about Plagwitz is that there are a lot of old, empty buildings, and also all those industrial buildings (Sven, 19).

Rather than seeing Leipzig's socialist past as wholly problematic and in need of eradication, participants such as Sabine felt that some of the sites connected with that past lent the city character and made it special:

Building sites.

Because I'm not from Leipzig I notice, when I go somewhere by tram, that there is still a lot of GDR advertising. Well, that's something I find cute...And then there are the high rises in the city centre...and then all the steel stuff and stuff like that, which isn't from now (Sabine, 18).

The fact that she finds symbols of the GDR 'cute' indicates a certain distance and exotic relation to this past. Yet, she also integrates aspects of it into her own identity and marks it as worth protecting lest Leipzig lose its specificity.

Concluding thoughts

Young people's daily lives in the city of Leipzig are characteried by both processes of de-territorialization and re-territorialization. On the one hand, their city has been subject to large-scale transformations in infrastructure, architecture, function, use and social structure over the past two decades. With these transformations, young people's own use of urban space and their attachments to it have changed, while pressures on them as individuals to be mobile and flexible in an unstable labour market have added to the sense of displacement and loosening of local ties. On the other hand, their spatial practices continue to be shaped strongly by daily routines that are in part a reflection of the institutionalization of young people's lives, yet also hold potential for niches of unsupervized (in)activity. These routines are embodied practices through which connections to the city are made 'on the move' and not through 'roots', as is so often implied in debates about footloose cosmopolitans and place-trapped locals.[30] Both young people's daily urban practices and their imagined present and future lives unfold along intersecting temporal and spatial scales. The city offers them opportunities for trans-national connections[31] that may be experienced as both enriching and threatening, while aspects specific to the city continue to lend a sense of place, be it the urban quarter, the spectacular centre, historical architectures, remnants of the GDR past or even derelict spaces and building sites. Rather than reiterating the contrast between locality and globality in our analyses of post-socialist transformation, we thus need to pay careful attention to the ways in which both are articulated in actual socio-spatial practices. At the same time, we need to consider which opportunities and restrictions arise from their intersection for unequally positioned groups within society. This means not only recognizing that young people experience age-related disadvantages, but also that their engagements with the trans-national city will be shaped by social inequalities.

Kathrin Hörschelmann lectures in Geography at the University of Durham.

Notes

1. See Nayak, A. and Kehily, M. J. (2006), 'Gender Undone: Subversion, Regulation and Embodiment in the Work of Judith Butler', *British Journal of Sociology in Education*, 27:4, pp. 459–472; Gregson, N. and Rose, G. (2000), 'Taking Butler Elsewhere: Performativities, Spatialities and Subjectivities', *Environment and Planning D: Society and Space*, 18: 4, pp. 433–452; cf Butler, J. (1990), *Gender Trouble. Feminism and the Subversion of Identity*. London and New York: Routledge; Butler, J. (1993), *Bodies that Matter. On the Discursive Limits of 'Sex'*. London and New York: Routledge.

2. See Jackson, P. (1998) 'Domesticating the Street: The Contested Spaces of the High Street and the Mall' in N. R. Fyfe (ed.) *Images of the Street. Planning, Identity and Control in Public Space.* London: Routledge, pp. 176–191; Vanderbeck, R. and Johnson, J. (2000) 'That's the Only Place Where You Can Hang Out': Urban; McRobbie, A. (2000) *Feminism and Youth Culture.* London and New York: Routledge; Crouch, D. (1998) 'The Street in the Making of Popular Geographical Knowledge', in N. R. Fyfe (ed.) *Images of the Street. Planning, Identity and Control in Public Space.* London: Routledge, pp. 160–175.

3. Noble, G. (2005) 'The Discomfort of Strangers', *Journal of Intercultural Studies* 26:1/2, pp. 107–120; Hage, G. (1997) *White Nation: Fantasies of White Supremacy in a Multicultural Society.* Annandale: Pluto Press.

4. Amin, A. and Thrift, N. (2002) *Cities. Reimagining the Urban.* Cambridge: Polity and Oxford: Blackwell, p. 29.

5. Dürrschmidt, J. (1997)'The Delinking of Locale and Milieu. On the Situatedness of Extended Milieux in a Global Environment', in: J. Eade (ed.) *Living the Global City. Globalization as Local Process.* London and New York: Routledge, pp. 56–72.

6. Amin, A. and Thrift, N.(2002) *Cities. Reimagining the Urban.* Cambridge: Polity and Oxford: Blackwell p. 77.

7. Andrusz, G., Harloes, M. and Szelenyi, I. (1996) *Cities after Socialism. Urban and Regional Change and Conflict in Post-Socialist Societies.* Oxford, UK and Cambridge, US: Blackwell.

8. Stadt Leipzig (2007) http://www.leipzig.de/int/en/stadt_leipzig/stadtentw/wirtschaft/, accessed 21/09/07.

9. Smith, F. (1998) 'Between East and West: Sites of Resistance in East German Youth Culture' in T. Skelton and G. Valentine (eds.) *Cool Places: Geographies of Youth Culture.* London and New York: Routledge, pp. 289–304.

10. Pilkington, H., Omel'chenko, E., Flynn, M., Bliudina, U., and Starkova, E. (eds.) (2002) *Looking West? Cultural Globalization and Russian Youth Cultures.* Pennsylvania: The Pennsylvania State University Press.

11. Evans, K.. (2002) 'Taking Control of Their Lives? Agency in Young Adult Transitions in England and the New Germany', *Journal of Youth Studies*, 3, pp. 245–269; Hörschelmann, K. (2008) 'Transitions to Work and the Making of Neo-Liberal Selves – Growing up in (former) East Germany' in A. Smith, A. Stenning and K. Willis (eds.) *Social Justice and Neoliberalism: Global Perspectives*, London: Zed Books, (forthcoming).

12. Katz, C. (2002) 'Stuck in Place: Children and the Globalization of Social Reproduction', in: R. Johnson, P. J. Taylor and M. J. Watts (eds), *Geographies of Global Change*, pp. 248–260; Katz, C. (2004) *Growing up Global: Economic Restructuring and Children's Everyday Lives.* Minneapolis: University of Minnesota Press; Katz, C. (2006) 'Power, Space and Terror: Social Reproduction and the Public Environment' in S. Low and N. Smith (eds.), *The Politics of Public Space.* New York and London: Routledge, pp. 105–121.

13. Katz, C. (2006) 'Power, Space and Terror: Social Reproduction and the Public Environment' in S. Low and N. Smith (eds.) *The Politics of Public Space.* New York and London: Routledge, pp. 111, 115.

14. Tomlinson, J. (1999), *Globalization and Culture*, Cambridge and Oxford: Polity Press and Blackwell.

15. Qvortrup, J. (1994), *Childhood Matters*, London: Ashgate.

16. James, A., Jenks, C. and Prout, A. (1998), *Theorizing Childhood*, New York: Teachers College Press; Valentine, G. (2003) 'Boundary Crossings: Transitions from Childhood to Adulthood', *Children's Geographies* 1, pp. 37–52.

17. Roberts, K., Clark, S. C., Fagan, C., and Tholen, J. (2000), *Surviving Post-Communism. Young People in the Former Soviet Union.* Cheltenham: Edward Elgar; Ilynski, I. (1995) 'The Status and Development of Youth in Post-Soviet Society' in J. Riordian, C. Williams and I. Ilynski (eds.) *Young People in Post-Communist Russia and Eastern Europe.* Aldershot: Dartmouth, pp. 11–28.
18. Smith, A. and Rochovská, A. (2008) 'Domesticating Neo-Liberalism: Everyday Lives and the Geographies of Post-socialist Transformations, *Geoforum,* in press.
19. ESRC R000223955.
20. Hörschelmann, K. and Schäfer, N. (2007) ''Berlin is Not a Foreign Country, Stupid!' – Growing up 'Global' in Eastern Germany', *Environment and Planning A*, 39:8, pp. 1855–1872.
21. Hörschelmann, K. and Schäfer, N. (2005) 'Performing the Global through the Local – Young People's Practices of Identity Formation in former East Germany', *Children's Geographies* 2, pp. 219–242.
22. Hörschelmann, K. and Schäfer, N. (2007) ''Berlin is Not a Foreign Country, Stupid!'– Growing up 'Global' in Eastern Germany', *Environment and Planning A*, 39:8, pp. 1855 – 1872.
23. Bourdieu, P. (1984) *Distinction: a Social Critique of the Judgement of Taste.* London: Routledge and Kegan Paul.
24. Beck, U. (2002) 'The Cosmopolitan Society and its Enemies', *Theory, Culture and Society,* 19, pp. 17–44.
25. cf.Vanderbeck, R. and Johnson, J. (2000) 'That's the Only Place Where You Can Hang Out': Urban.
26. Jackson, P. (1998)'Domesticating the Street: The Contested Spaces of the High Street and the Mall' in N. R. Fyfe (ed.), *Images of the Street. Planning, Identity and Control in Public Space.* London: Routledge, pp. 188–189.
27. Ruddick, S. (1996) 'Constructing Difference in Public Spaces: Race, Class and Gender as Interlocking Systems', *Urban Geography,* 17:2, pp. 132–151; Valentine, G. (1996) 'Children Should Be Seen and Not Heard: The Production and Transgression of Adults' Public Space', *Urban Geography* 17:3, pp. 205–220; cf. Lees, L. (1998) 'Urban Renaissance and the Street: Spaces of Control and Contestation' in N. R. Fyfe (ed.), *Images of the Street. Planning, Identity and Control in Public Space.* London: Routledge, pp. 236–253.
28. Lees, L. (1998) 'Urban Renaissance and the Street: Spaces of Control and Contestation' in N. R. Fyfe (ed.), *Images of the Street. Planning, Identity and Control in Public Space.* London: Routledge, p. 37.
29. The loss of those close relationships through moving to another part of the city was accompanied for Tom by isolation and disorientation. Finding new friends in his apartment block proved difficult and he thus relied increasingly on school for making new contacts. After school, this meant that he spent most of his time alone at home.
30. Hannerz, U. (1990) 'Cosmopolitans and Locals in World Culture', in M. Featherstone (ed.) *Global Culture.* London: Sage, pp. 237–252; Hannerz, U. (1996) *Transnational Connections.* Routledge: London and New York; Bauman, Z. (1998) *Globalization. The Human Consequences.* Cambridge: Polity Press; Tomlinson, J. (1999), *Globalization and Culture.* Cambridge and Oxford: Polity Press and Blackwell.
31. Amin, A. and Thrift, N. (2002) *Cities. Reimagining the Urban.* Cambridge: Polity and Oxford: Blackwell.

8

New Social Order and Change in Media Landscape

Hrach Bayadyan

In recent years we have had numerous opportunities to address the transformations of the urban spaces of Yerevan, specifically connecting these processes with the formation of new power relations in the post-Soviet Armenian nationstate. However, equally radical changes have occurred in the sphere of information technologies; television, radio and the print media. In the meantime the Internet has been, to a certain degree, turned into a communicative domain serving a variety of ends: it is already possible to identify a number of network services, different forums and communities as well as websites that claim the status of Internet portals. The transformations are still in progress. In the last two or three years new entertainment magazines have come out: they are both a novelty for the information sphere in Armenia and underline tendencies of social and cultural transformations. Meanwhile, the language and particularly, the status of the Armenian language has changed. It will not be an exaggeration to assume the spread of consumerist culture to be one of the crucial factors conditioning the formation of new social relations and social norms, new cultural values and codes of communication in post-Soviet Armenian society.

My aim here is to discuss the current media-situation not only and not so much against the backdrop of the global expansion of information and communication technologies, but to address it in the context of local socio-historical conditions, to understand it within the flow of radical political, economic, social and cultural transformations. On the other hand, the current state of the media not only reflects various manifestations of these transformations but also, step by step, engages itself with the very process of shaping cultural, social and other phenomena.

In this chapter I will attempt to examine social spaces of communication – the urban environment and traditional as well as new media (such as the Internet) through the following key question: given the condition of extreme social inequality and fragmentation how was it possible to find some social connectivity and stability in Armenia after radical social changes (collapse of the Soviet Union, the war in Karabagh, etc)? Perhaps this general question can be divided into more specific ones (even though I will be unable to touch upon all of them within the scope of this article): what are the principles for the formation of cultural codes that enable current social communication? What is the logic behind the choice of certain values over others? How past individual and collective conceptions are transformed under the pressure of new conditions, and etc? Finally, this general question can be reformulated: what has become of the Soviet modernity project in the Republic of Armenia since new collective and individual expectations and exhaustion of the energy of modernization can be felt in all spheres?

The urban environment

The transformations of the urban space of Yerevan have long been discussed. One of the key issues addressed has been the café construction boom at the expense of public spaces as well as the expansive plan of regeneration of the city centre (destruction or relocation of old buildings and the construction of Northern Avenue, etc). To clarify my point, I would like to start my story from an earlier period, from the so-called 'dark and cold years'.

What happened in Yerevan in the mid-1990s can be described as the de-urbanization and corrosion of the urban structures of the social space: a complex process manifested through the disintegration of transportation and heating infrastructures. And if we consider that the Soviet urbanization processes (especially for bigger cities) were tightly connected with industrialization and the formation of specific classes and cultures, then the total destruction of industry in post-Soviet times will complete the picture.

One of the most typical features of de-urbanization at the time was the loss of 'room temperature'. In the Soviet years it was common to place one of two possible instructions on pharmaceutical products: 'Keep in a dark, cool place' or 'Keep at room temperature'. In those years these two instructions were identical in our 'cool and dark rooms'. One of the main features of a Soviet (capital) city -"the room temperature" (if we borrow the expression from Soviet years) disappeared. More of a social than a technological phenomenon which differentiated the urban flat from a rural traditional hearth, it was the invisible witness of society's level of modernization.

Yerevan, with its population of more than one million, was deprived of central heating for several years. Consequently, when people got used to heating their homes with wood and kerosene heaters, a heavy layer of industrial and transportation smog which had hung over the city, common for the last Soviet decade, was replaced by the smoke coming out of chimneys of city flats generating a strange but mainly an ominous scene. It goes without saying that in the condition of electrical power shortages newspapers, television and radio were operating with an entirely different schedule. The expression 'mass media' became meaningless. Moreover, information foundations for the imagined public unity or, if we borrow Benedict Anderson's term, 'imagined communities', were shattered. This was a part of the process of gradual deterioration of overall communicative links when rituals, habits and beliefs, as well as norms and values uniting any given community (public), became meaningless.

Re-urbanization, or...?

An apparent sign of re-urbanization can be considered the completion of the road construction project of the city centre in the beginning of the 2000s. It is noteworthy that the financial resources from the Lincy Foundation were initially intended for business projects but eventually served the regeneration of the city centre. This way the government managed to use the resources of a diaspora Armenian donor more efficiently since the re-construction of the city centre served several aims at once. The direct positive impact of this project on the government's image was apparent. Nevertheless, more important was the re-evaluation of the city centre from the aspects of both fostering the continuous growth of real estate prices and private enterprizes and the development of the entertainment industry. Consistent privatization of the public space that has been resisted by social masses, seemed to be immediately legitimized. This provided an impetus for the emergence of an urban elite as well as lifestyles, places and heroes, habits and signs that demanded their ways and methods of representation, which did not fail to follow.[1] Now was the time for constructing 'elite buildings'. This turning point for post-Soviet society crowned the brilliant culmination of legitimization of the upper class and its illegally accumulated wealth during the first years of independence. The path of societal development, which up until that point could be suggested as only one of the possible paths, was already a fact.

But this is yet one side of the coin. The problem was not only the fact that re-urbanization was taking place with amateur methods and serving exclusively the powerful and the wealthy. The new transportation system in Yerevan, for example, constituted exclusively by private 'traffic lines' of mini-buses, originated on entirely new economic and social foundations. Up until now, we didn't have what we used to call in Soviet times a 'bus stop'. The essential problem is that the dimension of modernity in society is being totally lost. In a country previously claimed to be 'industrial', there is no industry, and is not foreseen to be in the near future. High culture continues to exist at the expense of the power's populism only. Moreover, re-urbanization is taking place at the expense of modernity's overall retreat, with the loss of its symbolic dimension and the exploitation of the energy of national-Soviet modernization. The privatization and utilization of public spaces of the 'Round-Shape' park can serve as an example. A good instance of the utilization of modernity's spatial and symbolic resources is the conversion of the area surrounding the *National* Theatre for Opera and Ballet (I want to stress the National) into an entertainment zone. Indeed, Opera is a symbol of modernity projects for every nation-state, and surrounding it with entertainment venues, does not only de-sacralize the Freedom Square (and eradicates the political meaning of the pan-national movement of the late 1980s) but is yet another expression of the wish to reassert that signs of modernity are 'a waste of time'. It is also an instance of negation or disregard of ambitions for modernity and of the readiness to cash in its symbolic resources.

If we summarize: if in the last few years a process of re-urbanization took place in the centre of Yerevan, it was not accompanied by re-modernization. What we have witnessed was re-urbanization, without, or more precisely, at the expense of modernization. Some remnants of the Soviet modernity project, even if they were not meant to disappear quickly, as it turned out, did not have an exchange value in the global market. Those were consumed in the local market with local enthusiasm and prudence.

Public and private TV

It is not my goal to present the chronology of changes in mass media. The first post-Soviet years are known as the best years of Armenian mass media. However, 'the romantic' period of the media's freedom lasted until the government realized that media can first of all serve as an ideological tool. Thus, it was governmental priorities and financial pressures rather than legislative and progressive post-Soviet regulations that defined post-socialist Armenian media. Therefore, we can assume that even if there were certain legislative 'gestures' towards democratic norms and 'European standards', practically the whole sphere of television broadcasting is controlled by the government. It is merely the mechanisms of control that have changed.

It has already been five years since state television was turned into public TV. Nevertheless, this public TV is totally controlled from the presidential palace, and serves the power's interests. It is almost completely deprived of a political dimension and is unjustifiably (for its status as public TV) commercial and entertainment oriented. Intellectual debates and plurality of political opinions are intolerable here and the elementary responsibility of TV to satisfy the public interest is ignored. Moreover, Armenian public TV has adopted the role of the main disseminator of consumer culture and propagator of slang.

Practice of private television is being regulated through the establishment of the National Committee of Radio and Television (2001) which has become a convenient tool for restructuring and controlling the field. At present, Armenian FM radio stations are mainly commercial. Plurality of opinions is tolerated only in printed media but the social significance of the latter is small, particularly due to its negligible circulation numbers.

Promises of the Internet

As it should by now be clear, I am not discussing 'the public sphere'. I am not attempting to question its relevance for the post-Soviet Armenian reality. Thus, it is not my intention to clarify whether Armenian mass media can or can not be considered as a public sphere. It might seem that the shrinkage of public space in the city could have been compensated for with opportunities provided by the media, if different groups and communities tried to regain the lost spaces through the media. However, as I have already argued, the mass media is controlled or is not open for political participation while the Internet is accessible only to a minority. Nevertheless, it is important to discuss the Internet, since it is a phenomenon that appeared after the collapse of the Soviet Union, under new conditions, and is seemingly less charged with the heritage of the Soviet past. The emergence of contemporary information and communication technologies in Armenia coincided with the overall post-Soviet crisis. That is why these technologies inevitably appeared and gained meaning in the context of several problems, such as mass immigration, re-construction of the collapsed economy, establishment of international collaboration, European integration, resolution of regional conflicts, recuperation of social solidarity and etc.

If we try to examine the arguments brought up by one of the most prominent advocates of the Internet as a public sphere, Mark Poster, we will be confronted with the fact that none of these arguments hold in the case of 'the Armenian Internet.'[2]

Despite the fact that in the last years we have seen a proliferation of easily accessible Internet points or clubs in Yerevan, full public accessibility still remains to be achieved. Part of accessibility is having adequate knowledge and skills, which is far from the case now. The limited availability of Armenian-language content and the absence or scarcity of the necessary software to store, process and retrieve Armenian-language content (translation programs, search engines, etc.) also poses a serious problem.

It is common to blame ArmenTel (Armenian telecommunication operator) for such problems, but the lack of a national strategy for IT development is an issue, too. Moreover, the national government's policies are directly preventing developments in this sphere, namely the expansion of its social significance. It is broadly known that the Armenian government's interest in the development of the software industry is chiefly for exports. Such orientation largely prevents the development of an internal IT market as well as the formation of a social need for IT and IT services.[3] Ironically, the only benefit from the government's actions was the expansion and proliferation of Internet information and news sources under the condition of the government's strict control over the broadcast media. Nevertheless, we should never overestimate the social significance of the former.

New printed media: entertainment magazines
I have already discussed the ambiguous state of the print media; on the one hand its position as the only source for expressing anti-governmental sentiments and on the other hand, its limited circulation and demand combined with minimal social significance. Nevertheless, even within these circumstances for almost three years we have witnessed the emergence of entertainment magazines, and their amount is still continuing to grow. *Afisha* (in Russian), *Gorod* (in Russian) and *El-Elite Life* (in Armenian) are among these. Since 2005 *Yerevan* monthly has been circulating. Herein, I will present several conclusions drawn from the small research I have conducted. First of all, I would like to clarify that these magazines are spontaneous phenomena, not yet economically justified. As opposed to several popular newspapers, these magazines have no oppositional or anti-governmental position. Even though it is hard to notice the official power's direct participation or commissioning, these magazines clearly serve to stabilize and reinforce the existing social order. Hence, we may suppose that publication of these periodicals

is an outcome of certain processes, though we can not exclude the possibility of a chance. One way or another, a certain tendency can be outlined; there are emerging entertainment magazines that are much more expensive than newspapers, have rather high print-quality and a specific orientation (entertainment, amusement and everything connected to these). I suppose that these magazines confirm my assumption about the emergence of a new urban situation in the centre of Yerevan.

These magazines round up the processes of privatization of space, creation of entertainment zones and the transformation of the city centre. Simultaneously, they reassert the government's policy of turning consumption into a dominant ideology and consumer values into the main tools for establishing cultural hegemony. It is implicit that the entertainment industry can not form and develop in any given culture without mass media, including print media. The construction of identities (personal and collective) of newly formed classes inevitably demands representation. We witness the proliferation of new environments, events, people, objects and new modes of entertainment calling for attention. New 'heroes' are being represented in new circumstances. On the one hand, there is a visualization of the situation (in a new style, gradually appropriating tools and techniques of representation) and on the other hand there is the cultivation and education of the viewer-reader's gaze. For instance, in an imaginary photo-story (El-Elite Life) different 'elite' places, such as restaurants, hotels, and shops are being connected to each other and, both separately and as a whole, given a meaning. This is also the way in which the elite is being defined: they are now primarily associated with wealth rather than the intelligentsia, as in Soviet years. Criteria are constantly changing; what is contemporary, elite, desirable, pleasant and worthy of duplication and how the 'new" youth, the rich, the intellectual, the entertained, the fashionable and the one appearing fashionable should be...

Transformations in language

In Soviet Armenia the Armenian language had an ambiguous status. Primarily due to compulsory secondary education, the dramatic rise of the level of literacy had an unprecedented empowering social effect for literary eastern Armenians. Vis-a-vis the fact that the language of the governing elite and some of the intelligentsia was Russian, the everyday languages of the rural population were the local dialects while in Yerevan the urban jargon, 'rabis' or 'the mafia language', had a socially influential role. Nevertheless, especially during the years of stagnation the endeavour of the Soviet government to russify national cultures, and spread the Russian language and culture as the language and culture of all Soviet people, was obvious. The post-Soviet history of the literary language with its ups and downs, new challenges and unforseen perspectives, is complicated and controversial enough not to allow us to arrive at simple conclusions. However, it is still not difficult to notice some current tendencies; the continuous spread of English, return to Russian in many spheres and the proliferation of extra-literary, colloquial new linguistic formations and class jargons.

The difficulty of having Armenian-language services and content on the web, that I have briefly touched upon above, is only one of the problems. There haveappeared new modes of public usage of language as well as linguistic domains that exist to satisfy the demands of communication environments, identities and communities formed around and by the media. The spread of mobile phones is another influential factor, though it is too early to make assumptions about their effects. The languages of FM radio, DJs, e-mail correspondence still carried out mainly with latin characters, Internet chat-rooms and forums as well as the language of translated video films and the jargon-language of entertainment TV shows, comprise the unprecedented manifestation of the 'secondary vernacularism'[4] of contemporary Armenian.

The retreat of Soviet modernization in a recently independent country should not seem paradoxical in the age of globalization when the foundations of nation-states and especially the abilities to master the fate of the national culture, are shattered. Nevertheless, in the context of Manuel Castell's ideas of the crucial significance of language in the survival of 'small cultures' in the age of information technologies,[5] it is not irrelevant to ask how we should name these rapid transformations of language. Shall we identify the fate of the national language with the literary langue or is the vitality of language precisely in its ability to revive in different spheres of application? Generally speaking, if the present social order rests upon the consummation of modernity's resources and its delegitimization, then a similar thing would happen to the literary language; the loss of the achievements of modernity would also mean the retreat of the literary language. However, what I conditionally call the official project of language, is more than the retreat of language. I hold that in the principle of current social solidarity (even if such solidarity has never been explicitly formulated), one can observe the deflation of literary eastern Armenian (if not its complete negation) and that of the social values, institutions of social legitimization and symbolic power attached to it. The legitimization of those using the urban jargon; the semi-literate and semi-criminal nouveau riches by, for example, giving them access to the parliament, has the purpose of erasing previous ideals and establishing new ones associated with the new power. From this point of view, it seems that the complicity of this government with that language could not be avoided.

On the other hand we can discuss the absence of language as an intellectual 'project', even though there is no need to put these (imaginary) projects on the same level, especially because, in the second case, the discourse involves the absence of a project. The word intellectual does not necessarily entail a unified concept of the intelligentsia. Reflecting upon the absence of any serious intellectual project, nevertheless, we should ask ourselves which kind of intelligentsia should we have expectations of: the conservative official intelligentsia or from those who have penetrated the political arena as an oppositional force? Or is it perhaps, the obligation of different marginals who hide themselves in obscure corners? The discussion of this remarkable question of the absence of an intellectual project, remains outside of the scope of this paper.

In the age of globalization in the context of the political and economic future of a nation-state, the obvious decrease of state nationalism (in terms of modernity), which in the case of Armenia runs parallel with the increasing rhetoric of national ideology on the level of the state, is explainable in current conditions of having a corrupt government with a commitment to obey the dictat of transnational capital. Here the dissipation of modernity is an important element in establishing a new social order and legitimizing new social classes. The devaluation of the literary eastern Armenian language is the logical consequence of these processes.

Conclusions

In the last years we have been witnessing legitimization of the emerging post-Soviet upper class and their wealth, which takes place along direct or indirect appropriation of power on their part. This is a curious process through which the crisis of government's legitimacy is 'overcome' through legitimizing illegitimate wealth. This alliance (of wealth and power) is establishing a model of a social order which is reinforced by the absolute domination of consumer values and norms. Certainly, this does not mean that Armenian society, where more than half of the population is poor, has become a consumer society. Here we can observe the strengthening positions of power and private capital at the expense of public interest and the values of civil society.

The simultaneously emerging culture, however we may prefer to name it, is highly dependent upon the mass media and information technologies. New cultural practices are being formed also in technological environments through various types of information and communication media. In a society that has been divided for many years, now certain social layers unite around new values and norms. New communities, relations, experiences and modes of behaviour are being constructed. The forms of social connections, individual and collective identities often come into being and are supported by the media. Thus, social transformations are both reflected in the significant changes in communication spaces and take place with the participation of different mass medias.

My observations about communication spaces can be summarized in the following way: urban spaces in Yerevan are largely privatized and handed over to the entertainment industry. Traditional electronic media (first of all public TV) are both massively controlled and unapologetically entertaining. To become a communication space the Internet has to overcome many technological, social and other obstacles.

Hrach Bayadyan is a cultural theorist researching media and postcolonialism in Yerevan, Armenia.

Notes

1. For a more detailed analyses about urban changes in Yerevan, see 'Tesaranner ev Nshanner Yerevani Poghotsnerum' (in Armenian). *Mshakuyt ev Technologia,* Yerevani Petakan Hamalsarani hratarakchutyun: Yerevan, 2003.
2. Poster, Mark. (2001) 'Cyber Democracy: The Internet and the Public Sphere' in *The Information Subject.* London: Routledge.
3. Bayadyan, Hrach. (2005) *Jamanakakits teghekatvakan ev haghordakcakan technologianeri taratsumy ev zargatsumy Hayajstanum.* Noravanq: Yerevan.
4. W. Ong's expression describes the vernacular language that appeared in the age of electronic media, which is different from the preliterate language. Ong, Walter J. (1989) *Orality and Literacy: The Technologizing of the Word.* London: Routledge.
5. Castells argues: 'If nationalism is, most often, a reaction against a threatened autonomous identity, then, in a world submitted to cultural homogenization by the ideology of modernization and the power of global media, language, as the direct expression of culture, becomes the trench of cultural resistance, the last bastion of self-control, the refuge of identifiable meaning'.Castells, M. (1997) *The Power of Identity: The Information Age: Economy, Society, and Culture,* vol. 2, Oxford: Blackwell, p. 52.

9

REMOTE CONTROL: DANGERS AND DELIGHTS OF ARMENIAN TV SURFING

Vahram Martirosyan

Remote control is perhaps the most popular household utility in Armenia. It is not accidental that one of the newspapers advertizing TV programmes has been announcing on New Year's eve that during the holidays one will have the most precious visitor – the television. It is true that we are not unique. A folding table has been invented in the United States to enable one to eat while watching TV (it has its own name- 'TV table'). Our neighbouring Russians have their own tender name for TV – 'TVik' (телек).

Although less widespread, the opposite attitude also exists. The same Russians and Americans have another name for TV as well 'ящик', 'a box', with a hostile connotation. According to the definition of the enemy that I have not picked up from military text books but from intellectual Q&As circulating in the air, the enemy is a person, phenomenon or power that occupies a person's mind and attention *vis-a-vis* his/her own will. The euphemism 'box' implies this attachment; the attraction of one's attention involuntarily even if s/he does not have a TV. In this case one has to hear the noises coming from a neighbour's loud TV if the walls of the house are thin as usual. Or one can not avoid providing an ear for the retelling of TV stories by others, which is perhaps even worse. Both attitudes towards TV can be explained. In the case with the folding table or 'telek' the average viewer feels him/herself to be the 'remote controller'. In the second case there is an intelligentsia, which feels hin/herself 'remote controlled' by the 'box'or 'yashchik', which denotes the word television in vernacular language.

In Soviet times the television was exercising its control so directly that if the news programme *Lraber* happened to criticize an official, the latter would be dismissed from his job (or the television would be commissioned to criticize, so there was an excuse to get rid of that official). Citizens did not even possess a remote control, and this would imply that one had to invest some physical effort to get up from his/her place to change the channel or to turn the TV off.

The expression 'It was told on TV...' belongs to the same era. This implies an abstract source without indicating the programme or the channel. This would be pointless anyway since there existed only two channels – the Armenian and the 'central' Moscow channel – both very similar to one another. For the majority, deprived of the critical faculty, the expression 'It was told on TV...' meant an expression of a 'higher' will, trustworthiness and legitimacy, while for a more aware minority it was an inversion of reality.

With perestroika it became officially permitted to present different contradicting opinions. Nevertheless, a multiplicity of opinions in Armenia, even during the post-totalitarian state, never found their roots. Perhaps the reason was our major force since between 1992 and 1995 due to electrical power shortages, there was no television. Like Carlson from the popular Russian cartoon, being occupied with the play of independence, we have touched a nerve, and television has stopped functioning as a mirror of reality. Thus, information was passed through orally, mythologized and turned into folklore. Only that...Even though in 2005 we celebrated the tenth anniversary of having an electrical power supply, the expression 'it was told on TV...' still persists.

Popular-unpopular

I have so far presented this paper as if I am the first to write about TV or the mass media. Since this is not the case, I would like to refer to a classic quote by Herbert Marshall McLuhan, famous for his expressions 'the global village' and 'the medium is the message'; television is itself the message.[1] However, if wepluralize this, on the one hand there are multiple messages (the majority of the Armenian population that inhabits the Ararat valley has access to around twenty channels, which makes the process of orienting oneself amongst this many channels resemblesan extreme sport – 'surfing'), on the other hand thousands of receivers armed with remote controls. Then how is it possible that the television (TV channels) and its assemblage – the box, manage to be so monotonous that the expression 'it was told on TV...' still persists?

In order to discuss these 'multiple messages' in a tenable manner, perhaps it makes sense to classify them under two genre-categories – information and entertainment. The study of our television communication networks demonstrates that entertainment shows are televised as much as ten times less than 'serious' programmes. As opposed to this, the ratings of entertainment shows are incomparably higher.

The above mentioned does not allow one to arrive at any conclusions since in Armenia the rating of the most viewed show is lower than the rating of the least viewed show in developed countries (these are the observations of the film director Ara Shirinyan). This means that there are no truly popular shows, and the (sea) surfer instead of reaching his/her favourite programme (wave), repeats the process or exits to the shore (turns the TV off). For the vast majority surfing does not have an alternative and it is not even clear in relation to what is being surfed.

This resembles a public boycott of TV stations. The word 'boycott' does not sound too extravagant in a country where the opposition has been boycotting parliamentary sessions and the referendum for constitutional amendments for several years. Nevertheless, we should also recall that there was a brief period of independent channels (1998–2001), and in a less tense political environment their rating was much higher than today's channels. There were news and political programmes competing with both entertainment shows and Russian popular channels.

Currently, a political parody that is between information and entertainment *Another Voice*, has somewhat higher ratings amongst the TV audience, while amongst informative-political programmes the popular ones are those that take a critical stance towards the official power ("Outline" – "Center" TV). However, there arises a question: why are these programmes so much further behind on the ratings scale than the shows containing vernacular jargon jokes (*Bernard Show* – Armenian TV) and jokes mocking the mentally ill (*The Abandoned*- Shant TV). This shows the level of (un)development in our society. How does the broadcast media reflect the dominant societal attitudes and moods of the opposition and its numerous followers and the ones disenchanted from corruption and bad governance?

Multiple-single

Political parody (*Another Voice*) is not entirely democratic since the prominent politicians parodied are in the end, as a rule, silenced by President Kotcharyan. Even in entertainment shows the hosts sooner or later betray the fact that they are presenting from the government's position (Petros Ghazaryan – *Outline*). Thus, all our TV stations present one-sided information and entertainment, and in total it is the rating percentage of one TV station that is distributed amongst approximately twenty channels. The question 'whose side are the channels taking' is a rhetorical one.

It is likely that someone will object that there is a certain degree of criticism in the air (even on public TV). Nevertheless, judging from the fact that criticism within the same channel has its fixed sphere and upper layer, we can assume that there has appeared a network of governmentally regulated television. I will call these NRTV (network of regulated television). All channels of NRTV get their share of 'criticism allowance'. Some channels are permitted to criticize the government, others the ministries. In a necessary instance for the official power, with its instructions and lists of persona non grata, one or two TV channels have a chance to be proud for airing oppositional politicians. On the lower level of the hierarchy there are those channels that can talk about beggars and garbage pickers. There are also those who voluntarily give up criticism for the sake of 'good news' (Yerevan, Armenia TV and its satellite channels, etc). Up until now, for reasons unknown to me, almost everyone is allowed to mock the ministry of foreign affairs and its minister. Two persons – Robert Kotcharyan and the prime minister Serge Sargssyan are outside of any criticism.

The scene described above might seem to have been inspired by a conspiracy theory. Nevertheless, besides expressing my feelings as a viewer, these are based on my personal experience as a journalist and especially on my shows *Revolution* and *The Club: Evening Readings* on channel The Center. Not long after my first broadcast, I was asked to give up *Revolution* 'without blood', replacing it with a Sunday informative analytical show with a wide range of criticism. At first glance, this seemed to be presenting me with an opportunity to say all that I was not licensed to say (like in Soviet times) between the lines, but in reality any type of deal with the government would mean a loss of journalistic independence. Eventually the *Revolution* as well as *The Club: Evening Readings* were closed down almost simultaneously with the closing down of Sergei Danielyan's *Barb Wire*, Vahram Sahakyan's *Right to the Face* and Violette Grigoryan's *Autograph* shows. At a certain moment the government undermined its own decision, probably exhausted from Europe s pressures, to cede The Center (in this case the name of the channel is symbolic) to the followers of the principles of free media and non-clichéd mentality. Only one or two newspapers highlighted the topic.

With regard to Philosophy, Wittgenstein draws parallels with orthography, which is to consider the orthography of the word 'orthography' itself.[2] The public evaluation of the importance of closing down a number of programmes was made difficult due to the paradox that the only truly mass media in Armenia – the television, which was supposed to reflect upon the boundaries of the freedom of speech and be amongst the vanguard of its defenders, has been deprived of this fundamental right.

It has been overly discussed but since the situation has not changed, it should be mentioned that one of the reasons for the public boycott of the television is that its economic status continues to remain independent from the number of viewers. Here as well, as in the case of political content, the primary commissioner is not society. Then, in what ways is the latter overlooked?

The public TV that serves exclusively to the government, thanks to a cunningly passed law, feeds both from the state budget and commercials. It charges the highest price for advertizing in the country putting private channels in an unequal position. Private channels, already financially bankrupt, have to compete not to please the audience but the Palace. This is due to the fact that in NRTVs' big commercial providers are distributed from above and are also under the government's heels. That is why when the government closes down an independent channel (as was the case with A1+ in 2001), other 'independent channels' announce that the reason it did not get frequency was an outcome of transparent and fair competition. This is the reason that journalists not enjoying officials' favour, who in other countries would be called 'stars', are not sought and professionals, who would always find ways to deliver the truth, are constrained within a narrow circle.

As a result since the closing down of the alternative news TV channel A1+, which also marked the end of the competition between A1+ and Ar for adopting a more oppositional stance between 1997 and 2001, there has been a great decline of criteria. Journalists of A1+ declared that they would not accept a proposition to work with any other TV channel for as long as their own channel is not allowed to air. Today, even if they try, they will not be able to find work on other channels. That is, any journalist whose political orientation differs from that of the government can no longer practice his/her profession.

There are TV channels that have been 'occupied' by oligarchs at the government's demand, so that the frequencies would not fall into undesirable, oppositional hands. They are in a specific, third situation. They also can not function according to a business logic: they would not win popularity since they are not free, are an outcome of a deal made with the government and can not expect a share from commercials distributed to NRTVs since they already have wealthy owners. They either pay their employees with 'natural products' (Ar and Hayreniq have a history of paying employees' salaries with cigarettes) or retroactively cut their salaries. They also steal the newspapers' share for advertizing by publishing ticker adds. The consequences of this simple self-preservation are unavoidable: Ar is rapidly descending on the rating scale while The Center gradually loses its distinctivefeatures.

The main rule of the advertizing market has long been 'dumping' which caused the proliferation and price decrease of commercials. Sometimes, as viewers like to joke, programmes are not interrupted by commercials but commercials by programmes. The same sequence of 'elite' furniture, worn-down cars, flats and jewellery can last for hours. Perhaps it is the dictat of the overall environment that in commercials the rhetoric of 'European quality' is necessarily interrupted by the enumeration of 'national values'. The eloquent but illiterate language sometimes results in propaganda for cannibalism, such as 'Armenian grape with an angry containment and taste of a Cilician man' (wine factory's ad) or absurd phrases such as 'he will go back to those who will come' (Casino Cleopatra). Under the conditions when the public is supplied neither with information nor entertainment, it is being flooded with consumer goods, and driven to commodity fetishism. While low income does not even allow for the formation of a consumer society (that analysts often warn against) but conserves us on the level of a consuming society. I am using the word 'even' since, as the experience of the West has proven, a consumer society at least provides good resources for critical self-reflection.

Nevertheless, there is a certain degree of subversion allowed as long as it does not oppose the government. In the past only one and today already two channels exclusively broadcast Soviet films (Hayreniq, Ar), thus injecting nostalgia towards the communist dictatorship. This is a complete puzzle if we consider that the owner of these channels is an oligarch who could neither have wealth nor television channels back in those times. The only assumption to be made is that he wants communism for the poor, so that the latter is no longer dependent upon his tax money, and capitalism for himself. To save money Soviet and sometimes foreign films are shown so repetitively that the viewer finds him/herself in the position of the protagonist from *Groundhog Day* who constantly wakes up on the same day. The idealization of the Soviet past is interrupted with a contemporary commercial of rusted tobacco leaves. On a TV channel belonging to an oligarch (whether they have ideological ambitions or not), the air time for commercials is dedicated to praising its owner and his business, even though an average viewer can not always identify the person due to the fact that often legal and actual owners are different.

The case of ALM (Alternative Media) is completely unique. Here political shows are entertaining: the arsenal of facts and arguments used by its hosts and anchors are exclusively amateur and populist (This is reminiscent of Shukshin's story *Thrown Away* about a false wise-man of the village). Entertainment shows gain a political resonance (*Stars*) when they are aimed at wide public consumption and guided by the standards of home video. This creates an effect of a reality show (*Cube, Alfred's Room*, international equivalents are *Loft Story* and *Big Brother*) which can be useful for our society's self-awareness but also destructive in that it degrades the television's function since this is not a conscious outcome of an intended project. In this sense ALM in reality is an alternative to the media. Perhaps Ar was a real alternative between 1997 and 1999 when even the titles of its programmes –*No Film, Centre of Inattention, The Life of Unknown People* revealed the channel's non-conformist stance and its opposition to what was official and traditional. The ridiculously disproportionate number of TV channels compared to the size of the audience results in limiting the function of channels to choosing the next talk-show's guest. This decreases the perceived significance of those events and persons that deserve presentation. As a result, the representation of public persons of a status wider than national is replaced by that of the capital, the latter by that of the scope of neighbourhood and so on. Remarkably, in politics it is the opposite: small players with mafia nick-names and modest intellectual abilities are occupying higher and higher positions.

The rarity of cultural programmes is common for all channels, which is strange if we consider the popular polemic that targets the 'national'culture. It is strange, since as the monotonous choir of artists and politicians asserts 'We should present ourselves to the world with our culture'. Relatively more attention is paid to culture in news programmes. Nevertheless, the reflections are limited to age-old pompousness and adjectives that have long lost their object (reminiscent of from Robert Musil's novel , *The Man without Qualities*). Here more than in other spheres, information itself is confused with the journalists' value judgements (normally very incompetent), without criteria and a definition of the discourse: average men and dilettantes are declared great. Criticism and critical-analytical insight are absent. A further factor is the air-time given to European football championships. One can surf through Shant's England, ArmenAkob's Germany, Armenia's Italy and HayTV's France, and completely lose one's own feelings of territorial identity when the public TV funded by tax payers, shows the Spanish championship. This is also an explicit expression of fetishism in sport which is typical for totalitarian regimes (it has been historically confirmed that it especially characterizes fascism and the Soviet dictatorship).

Possible-impossible

In the post-revolutionary restoration, in our case – *revanche*, when the power has been hijacked by the middle communist nomenclature, the Soviet model of having only one TV channel is the dream of those in power for reshaping the multi-channel field (thus, it betrays society's *axiome de crédibilité*, which is zero). The government is reshaping the field not in the physical sense by decreasing the quantity of TV channels, but by dictating their content since it is obliged to formally, even according to its legislation, follow western demands for democratization. Despite the fact that there have been adopted numerous laws and regulations on mass media and specifically television broadcasting, the tenders of TV and radio frequencies are totally dictated to by the government while 'unpleasant' companies are forced to leave the field.

The media policy of the current Armenian government is the attitude of the people of the crowd, (according to Baudrilliard 'the silent majority') which he calls 'neutralizing appropriation'.[3] Society deprived from public means of expression is in deep apathy since it can not influence the course of events. Post-Soviet developments in Armenia are the direct confirmation of the Nobel Prize winner Kenneth Arrow's 'theory of impossibility' according to which the mechanisms of democracy contain real cracks for dictatorship.[4] Society can not reform the law either, even though it is possible to apply the existing ones not according to the 'rules of clan competition'.

Hence, it has two alternatives: to survive until the next elections (but this will mean that society survives from election to election) or to wait patiently for the power to voluntarily respect the conditions it accepted from society (such as the legislation), which is practically impossible, or...revolution.

Vahran Martirosyan is a writer and journalist in Yerevan, Armenia. His most recent novel is Landslide (2007).

Notes

1. McLuhan, Marshall. (1994) *Understanding Media: The Extensions of Man* (1964). Cambridge: The MIT Press, p. 5.
2. Wittgenstein, Ludwig. (1999) *Philosophical Investigations* (1953). New Jersey: Prentice Hall, p. 57.
3. Baudrillard, Jean. (1983) *In the Shadow of the Silent Majorities, or, The End of the Social and Other Essays.* Foreign Agents Series. New York: Semiotext(e).
4. Arrow, Kenneth. (1963) *Social Choice and Individual Values* (1951). New York: Wiley.

SECTION FOUR: PUBLIC SPACES, TIMES AND SPHERES

10

TIME WITHOUT QUALITIES: CRACKING THE REGIME OF URGENCY

Stephen Wright

What is known as the public sphere has been the object of sustained and welcome reflection over the past decade. But does the term itself not somehow predetermine the very object it is supposed to describe? When one speaks of a public 'sphere', one makes use of a metaphorical term, which inadvertently predisposes the user to conceive of the public dimension in spatial terms, whereas what is primarily at stake when memory and forgetting well up in the present is less public space than public *time*. But what exactly *is* 'public time' and how might one conceptualize it? More pressingly, what is its status today at a time when new communications technologies as well as the generalization of flex-time in the labour market have come to imperil the very notion of *private* time? Breaking with romantic conceptions of the artist as outsider, sociologists have pointed out the extent to which artists represent in this regard the ideal-type of the worker of the future, whose work time never stops and never starts. How have artists drawn attention to the sort of disqualified, vacant or fuzzy time – time 'without qualities' – that might be described as public? Might one not think of public time as carving out breathing spots, intervals, transitory breaches in the very core of collective existence, time slots still unfettered by moral or political discipline? When one turns to practical examples of time-based art practices, often inscribed in the body politic or human landscapes – infiltration practices, tactical media initiatives – which unfold not only in space but in time, one is obliged to acknowledge that time is their defining but as yet entirely undefined factor.

My chapter has to do with cracks. With crevices, fissures, breaches, gaps and intervals. But above all with cracks. There's a crack, says songwriter and poet Leonard Cohen, a crack in everything. That's how the light gets in. Mystical overtones notwithstanding, this is an intriguing insight. For what is of interest to me here are the cracks in otherwise seamless time – and how they can be hacked. Time appears to us as a seamless continuum – and indeed to speak of cracking into time is to use a spatial metaphor to grasp time. Our phenomenological experience of time is such that we are invariably compelled to seek recourse to spatial metaphors to speak about it: though we can no more leave space than we can leave time, we are able to visually verify the fissuring of space; we can see and feel its discrepancies and qualities. This is not true of time, of course, though we are intuitively aware of the ill-fit between lived time and chronological time, we struggle to find the word-images to describe it. In a wonderful passage in W.G. Sebald's extraordinary novel, *Austerlitz*, the protagonist points out this conceptual difficulty. 'If Newton really thought that time was a river like the Thames, then where is its source and into what sea does it finally flow? Every river, as we know, must have banks on both sides, so where, seen in those terms, where are the banks of time? What would be this river's qualities, qualities perhaps corresponding to those of water, which is fluid, rather heavy, and translucent?' The Newtonian metaphor of time as a flow seems to cunningly postulate some timeless reality through which time moves. But perhaps it is that sometimes time flows through time itself; that there can be not only different quantities but different *qualities* of time. And what is of interest to me – following Robert Musil's wonderful lead – is a time without qualities. An available time, an *undisciplined* time, a public time, whose ideological and moral density is tolerably low.

Rather than focusing on the sort of monumental urban paraphernalia that ideologically demarcate our cityscapes, visual artists are often fond of those empty, unqualified spaces, which in English are called vacant lots, but are more eloquently known in French as *terrains vagues*: they are places in transition, inbetween zones in the urban fabric where it is positively possible to project difference. I am interested here in the temporal equivalent of these vague zones: vague intervals, breathing spaces in an increasingly frenetic regime of urgency. This regime is the key component of the privatization of the public sphere, not merely or even primarily because it transforms it into yet another commodity, but because it is premised on the indistinctness between public and private time. Lived experience is permanently on call, and where the private knows no limits, the public has no where to begin. In Jacques Ranciere's recent book, *The Hatred of Democracy*, he argues that democracy is never a given but always under construction – neither borne forth by any historical necessity nor the bearer of any – he insists that the sphere of democracy is the interval, forever to be re-conquered, between legal identity and social identity. And that sphere is essentially temporal: democracy is the process of struggle against the privatization (of the public sphere), the process of broadening the public sphere. The sort of public time that I refer to as without qualities – in other words, non-subjected to privatized usage – is the very condition of the possibility of democracy.

Yet today, time is increasingly and indeed massively qualified and quantified. We live under what some authors have described as the dictatorship of real time, a tyranny of the present, or a regime of urgency that defines our social time slots and roles. The dominant time metaphors that I hear myself using these days – and which led me to thinking about the need for a time without qualities – seem linked to verbs of possession, privatization and yield: *have* time, *lack* time, *lose time, save time.* As the philosopher Zaki Laïda writes, there is an interaction between the acceleration of globalization and a genuine redefinition of our relationship to time: everything is moving faster and this 'faster', so to speak, itself is felt all the more acutely in that it is linked to the perception that it is spreading worldwide. Globalization is experienced in the form of the tyranny of real time over real space, as if, in some way, the equalization of conditions of access to space by different actors...has shifted competition into the field of time. The point is no longer to gain new spaces, but to gain time. Or, to be still more precise, it is in gaining time...that one is able to regain new spaces (markets for business). World space is thus entirely temporalized. Being in world time comes down to being part of a new planetary dynamic and not belonging to any given space.

In other words, the advent of the regime of generalized urgency in economic life is closely linked to the emergence of this new worldwide space-time continuum.

The fate of public time should not be underestimated. Our societies are undergoing today a period of economic metamorphosis that may well culminate in the total commodification of lived experience, where the logic of capital will end up penetrating literally every aspect of life itself – of life as capital. Little by little, modern capitalism, based upon a wage-labour relationship – which though certainly ridden with conflict, nevertheless by acknowledging the separation of the contracting parties and by limiting the labourer's obligation to a certain amount of work, sets out jointly recognized and legally upheld boundaries between the sphere of labour and the sphere of private life, between working time and leisure time – has yielded to a new breed of capitalism, based upon the capture of the cognitive, creative and emotional capital of working subjects. Certain authors have acknowledged such key significance to the generalization of aesthetic and intellectual functions in the general economy that they have come to redescribe our contemporary mode of production as 'cognitive capitalism', not only because of what it produces (not so much objects *per se* as consumer-subjects of objects whose production has been outsourced to the global south and east) or through the systematic inclusion in commodity goods and services of cultural and communicational components. In its very mode of producing, the production process has been intellectualized, aestheticized and more insidiously still, *artialized*, as Montaigne usefully put it some four centuries ago.

Now, this new configuration begs the question as to how co-workers (to use fashionable neo-management jargon) can be totally 'mobilized'. How can their subjective involvement be maximized, and how can they be made to show unreserved identification to their job in the framework of a wage-labour relationship which is based upon an opposition between the subject and the company? As economist André Gorz has written in his recent book, *The Immaterial*, the total subsuming of the production of the self by capital runs up against limits which cannot be overcome as long as there subsists between the individual and the company, between labour and capital, a heterogeneity which enables the former to withdraw from the equation; to refuse total work.

Total work is a frightening prospect and the fact is that today the heterogeneity Gorz refers to is still solidly anchored in social mores – meaning that capitalism has a long term project of ideological attrition and subversion ahead of it if that heterogeneity is to be overcome. But in theory at least, and in many sectors of immaterial labour in practice, its objective is already perfectly clearly defined: wage-labour has to be abolished. Each person must become for him or herself a business, Gorz continues, and has to become, for him or herself, as labour power, a form of fixed capital that needs to be continually reproduced, modernized, broadened and recapitalized. No constraint can be imposed upon her/him from the outside; she/he must be her/his own producer, her/his own employer and her/his own seller, imposing upon herself/himself whatever constraints are necessary in order to ensure the viability and competitiveness of the *business which she/he is*.

Here we have a glimpse into entrepreneurial utopia: the genuine co-worker is none other than an entrepreneur, managing not only his career but his life, his relationship to himself and to others in the form of a small or medium sized business model. We also have a glimpse into the conflation of private and public time into a regime of total temporal mobilization – the dystopia of utterly qualified time.

Art, unfortunately, is all the less removed from this development in that in many respects it has been the laboratory for test-driving it; or as sociologist Pierre-Michel Menger recently asserted, its 'principle of fermentation', allowing management to appropriate what, until not so long ago, were skills specific and intrinsic to artistic activity – autonomy, creativity, high levels of involvement in an activity, not merely acceptance of flexibility and mobility but insistence upon them, non monetary remuneration, inter-individual competition, strategic exploitation of an unequal distribution of symbolic capital often referred to as 'talent' and so on.

Whereas outside working hours, workers were free (capital merely claiming the body of the worker for the duration of the working day), contemporary 'cognitive' capitalism has found ways to assert a claim to every aspect of being, but designating any part of that being as a resource. As McKenzie Wark puts it, in his *Hacker's Manifesto*, the struggle to limit the working day, while salutary as a means of freeing the body from commodity labour, no longer frees the worker from the commodity, but merely releases the subject as producer for the even more burdensome task of being the subject as consumer.

If we are to enjoy time without qualities, time itself must be freed from commodification and an economy of scarcity.

Stephen Wright is a theorist and researcher at L'Institut Nationale d'Histoire de l'Art, Paris.

11

PUBLIC SPHERES

Malcolm Miles

The disintegration of the Soviet Union in 1991 inflected the discourse of a public sphere in a particular way, drawing out contrasts between familiar and unfamiliar models of a public sphere to, perhaps, reveal difficulties in both. My purpose in this chapter is to problematize received ideas of the public sphere – in part to move from a normative use of the term *the* public sphere to a more contingent plural, public *spheres* – by drawing on cases which do not fit the norm. In part it is also, not to junk the idea of a public sphere, but to seek to recover its core values in a more open and realistic way. This may mean regarding a public sphere as ephemeral, a process rather than a civic identity aligned with certain kinds of urban spaces, and as spanning received divides of public and private realms (or public and domestic spaces). I retain, as a leap of faith, the idea of a public sphere in which members of a society determine its values and shape, themselves.

Points of departure

During the period of state-socialism, the public sphere was explicitly – in official terms – the state itself, with its apparatus of committees and other organs, including the security service. The state and the sphere of public determination were, logically, fused after the Revolution. The state enacted a popular revolutionary will, articulated by the people's party which formed the core of the state and was in effect successor to the revolutionary factory Soviets of 1917. Of course, even by the mid 1920s, under Stalin, the state had become an institutionalized form of the Revolution's continuity, with all the difficulties of institutionalized power (combined with a massive and rapid programme of industrialization and collectivization). To say now in retrospect, after the abuses of power, that the state was the form of the public sphere in the Soviet Union seems far-fetched, almost banal. The state did not wither away, but strengthened its mechanisms for perpetuation. An elite emerged, as might have been predicted from the strategy of a revolution led by a political avant-garde, or intelligentsia, and gradually became not an intellectual but a party elite fixated by power, a new establishment elaborating the end of history in such a way that it would not end. There were contradictions, clearly, not least in that admission that the ultimate post-revolutionary state had not been attained – as in the emergence of an abstract art read as allied to psychiatric disorder, when such disorders were the material product of a pre-revolutionary society – would undermine the basis of that state's ensconced power. Hence the abuses of the Stalinist period and the less dramatic dereliction of the Brezhnev period, so that the final disintegration in 1991 was not entirely a surprise to those within the system. It was simply that the means of expression of this realm of doubt was not politics but a distinctively cynical humour.

Yet there was hope once. Histories of the 1917 Bolshevik Revolution (and the gradual implosion of the Tsarist regime after the assassination of Alexander II in 1881[1]) show the evolution of state socialism as performance of the people's self-determination as a society. I introduce this as a trope, however, to provoke an equally sceptical approach to such other concepts of a public sphere as are available, including that derived from the model of Athenian democracy (to which I refer below). The difficulty as I read it is not the credibility gap of the Soviet Union, then, in contrast to the localized, informal and invisible public spheres which may have existed within it, but the inadequacy of more or less any claim that a genuine public sphere has existed in history except in cases which are historically marginal. These might include the ephemeral abolitions of office and property of millenarian groups in the medieval period.[2] But if such cases remain inspirational, if vaguely so, given how little we know of them, they offer little prospect of being mapped onto contemporary society in the period of globalization.

This is my real point of departure. I regard the mythicized public sphere of the West, often seen as beginning in the transactional society of Athens in the classical period, as no less fanciful a form of a public sphere than that of the Soviet Union. It is easier to say this today than before 1991, in the context of a triumph of market interests over even the principles of liberalism by which they were moderated in most European societies in the nineteenth and most of the twentieth century, notably in the post-1945 consensus of welfare provision. But even before 1991, the idea of a western public sphere appeared deficient in the persistence of widespread inequalities and divisions not only of access to wealth and health but also of race, class background, gender and age, and a disenfranchizement of groups within the dominant society which was by design rather than default. Time blurs histories, but as recently as the 1960s black people had to struggle for civil rights in the United States. In the 1960s, too, the United States (with British government support but not troops) attempted to prop up a corrupt regime in South Vietnam and justified the use of weapons of mass civilian death and environmental destruction (such as napalm) in the name of a fight against communism. The vehemence of the Cold War as fought by the West seems as irrational as the suppression of abstract art, say, in the Soviet Union. This suggests the second world, as defined at the time in contradistinction to the first world of the more affluent West, represented some shadow within the first world's political and social consciousness that the leaders of that world could not afford to allow to exist.

Against this background of oppositional dualism and internal contradiction, a counter-culture took shape from 1967 onwards, pointing to an evacuation of ethics within the West's most powerful state (and what was called 'the military-industrial complex'). For Joan Didion, 'All that seemed clear was that at some point we had aborted ourselves and butchered the job...'; hence, as disaffected young people gathered in the Haight-Ashbury district, 'San Francisco was where the social haemorrhaging was showing up...where the missing children were gathering and calling themselves "hippies"'.[3]

Perhaps the counter-culture, from the Summer of Love in 1967 to the 'Woodstock Festival' in 1968, then in anti-road protests in the 1990s, and recent anti-capitalist and environmentalist activism, constitutes another form of a public sphere in which groups marginal to the dominant society take the shaping of their own society into their own hands. This, too, can be mythicized, but a sphere of collaborative determination occurs in direct action. It may also erupt in moments of political transition when the power of a regime is sufficiently fractured to enable people to enact its demise, as by attacking its public monuments. The moment is brief, and old ideas and structures of power may be replicated, but attacks on public monuments reclaim the sites of a regime's public realm, making them suddenly sites of a public sphere demonstrating the inadequacies of such sites as a public sphere under the regime. Similarly, direct action re-defines public space as a site of militant occupation, no longer as a zone of monuments and public parks, or spaces for the leisure of middle class male society in which the values society as a whole is required to respect are represented in bland statues.

Perhaps there is an incremental public sphere, too, as movements for change gradually gain ground and minor advances contribute to what may become a shift of attitude and practice, hence of power. Green consumerism suggests this when people subscribe to organic vegetable box deliveries not only as a way to buy fresh food but also to belong to a network.[4] In Russia in the 1890s, too, new kinds of citizens' organizations arose in response to a rural famine and the Tsar's failure to deal with it. Orlando Figes writes that this contributed to an intellectual fashion for Marxism as a social science, and that urban middle class and professional feeling was thence channelled into projects for agronomy, health and education. He concludes, '... the whole of society had been politicized and radicalized as a result of the famine crisis.'; and that, 'From the 1890s can be dated the emergence of a civil society, a public sphere and an ethic, all in opposition to the Tsarist state.'[5] Here, a public sphere is aligned not with specific types of space but with an attitude of refusal, and with it implicitly an effort to reconstitute social organization more equitably and rationally. Figes writes with an agenda – stated in his title, *A People's Tragedy* – yet however much he loathes the state that emerged after 1924, and reads its origins in Leninist Marxism, his allusion to a public sphere of social agency among the intelligentsia (with liberal and radical wings), is helpful in understanding how socio-political shifts occur.

But is there a possibility for a non-oppositional public sphere that does not carry in its attitudes and tactics a counter-image of the oppression it seeks to overthrow, which it later replicates? What, metaphorically, would be its site? How would it act? This leads me to the theoretical work of

Henri Lefebvre, as a textual point of departure, and to his theory of moments of liberation within the routines of everyday lives.[6] Lefebvre is better known for his theory of space, in *The Production of Space,* published in French in 1974 and in English in 1991,[7] and interpreted by Edward Soja in *Thirdspace.*[8] But in his earlier work, prior to the events of May, 1968 in Paris, he outlines an idea that moments of sudden clarity and realization occur amid the dulling routines of work in a capitalist society, and are transformative. Perhaps, loosely, there is a similarity here with Joseph Beuys' idea that everyone has a creative imagination – is an artist in that sense – and can thereby imagine new social as well as aesthetic forms. Equally loosely, perhaps there is also a relation to Herbert Marcuse's idea of society as a work of art[9] (on which I write elsewhere).[10]

Before embarking on the enquiry, I need to insert a qualification: that, today, public space is increasingly privatized, often becoming a space for consumption in urban redevelopment schemes. While urban designers regard the provision of new public spaces as central to urban redevelopment schemes, then, this produces a simulacrum of public space in the ubiquitous urban piazza, denoting a fantasized latte-drinking society remotely informed by the public squares of cities such as Florence and Siena (which, presumably, architects visit on holidays) but in effect replacing public access with consumption in a globalized culture of brands. A defence of public space needs to be mounted, of course, but there is a difficulty in that such a defence may incorporate or consolidate an alignment of public spaces with a public sphere when this has not been the case. So, I reiterate, the public realm of a western city is usually a realm of representation to the mass public of the values they are required to serve, denoted by statues of (usually) men. It is a site of power's display, not self-determination. Today, urban design may take the place of statues, but historically the public realm, marked by exclusion by race, gender and class, is a device for social control.

If, then, sites of a public realm are aligned with the metropolitan public spaces in which institutional and administrative buildings were clustered from the eighteenth to the late twentieth century, the built form of those sites denotes the values and systems of ordering to which members of a society are required to conform. Only in revolt are these sites re-occupied to produce a public realm.

This gives me three categories which figure in the argument. First, public space as a material realm. Second, a public realm of monuments and social control. And third, a public sphere of social self-determination. By using a tripartite model – influenced by Henri Lefebvre's theories of spatiality – I avoid putting the historical public realm and the metaphorical public sphere in opposition, though I need to differentiate them. In all this my allegiance is to liberation -from the counter-culture but also anticipated in radical philosophy.[11] Herbert Marcuse writes, for instance, that beyond the limits of containment imposed by the established bourgeois order,

> '...there is also the space, both physical and mental, for building a realm of freedom which is not that of the present: liberation also from the liberties of exploitative order – a liberation which must precede the construction of a free society, one which necessitates an historical break with the past and the present.'[12]

But how is the break made and what follows? That is too large a question. My concern in this chapter is specifically with the relation of a public sphere to a public realm and public spaces and to the transitional or private spaces in which implicit social change occurs. It is also with the contrast between the performative character of occupations of public spaces, the monumental aspect of the public realm, and the intellectual idea of a public sphere.

Public Spaces

When privatized spaces encroach on public spaces, as when streets of common access and multiple use are developed as an outdoor mall, cultural district or heritage quarter in a city seeking to re-brand its image, a potential space of interaction tends to be lost. The unplanned and appropriated is replaced by the designed and prescribed. There is sociological evidence that groups of people such as the young and young unemployed use mall spaces for hanging-out, regardless of surveillance,[13] yet the provision of new public spaces in urban design projects seems like an admission of the loss of sites for public mixing. These sites are often decorated with public art, in a new imposition of conformity to the values (in this case aesthetic) of an elite (in the form of bodies such as the Arts Council) and denoting no less a power relation by shifting from history to art in the content of representation. Nor does locating statues of cultural figures at street level reduce conformity, in this context to the model of celebrity.

Cases of aestheticized public spaces include Centenary Square and Victoria Square in Birmingham, both public-sector projects, and Broadgate in London's financial district, a private-sector development. Hays Gallery is a vaulted mall newly built in heritage style with shops, cafés and a kinetic sculpture of an Elizabethan ship, on the recently gentrified south bank of the Thames near London Bridge. Artist Jochen Gerz sought to introduce the voices of members of diverse urban publics (through short texts applied to a circular bench) in The Public Bench, in Coventry in 2004, but the site itself is marginal; a gap between the cathedral and other kinds of spaces. In contrast to these examples, an ideological message is carried by Plaza del Fossar de les Moreres,[14] a small paved plaza near the church of S. Maria del Mar in Barcelona. Here, dirges are sung annually on 11 September – the national day of mourning – in memory of the martyrs of the city's fall to the Bourbons in 1714.

Plaza del Fossar is one of a hundred or so small open spaces created or modified in preparation for Barcelona's hosting of the 1992 Olympic Games. These are spread throughout the city's residential and business districts, in a public-centred planning regime. Alongside economic growth after fascist repression (from 1937 until 1975), cultural tourism in the city is aligned to the creation of a specifically Catalan cultural infrastructure.[15] This is evident in a new National Theatre, a new Theatre College, a new National Auditorium, and – for a global stage – a Museum of Contemporary Art. These public spaces and institutional buildings may constitute a refurnished public realm pointing towards a potentially new public sphere, contextualised also by, for instance, the reconstruction of Josep Sert's pavilion for the Spanish Republic from the 1936 Paris World Exposition. Across the road is a painted steel sculpture by Claes Oldenburg and Coosje van Bruggen, indicating a nod towards the global art market, but not far away are streets named after Rosa Luxemburg and Salvador Allende. But this is a unique context. Barcelona has a unique history and unusual infrastructure in which the public-sector led development until the mid 1990s, selling on sites to the private sector and ploughing back the profit into further renewal, following the model of progressive humanism of the 1859 plan for its northern extension (*Eixample*) by Idelfons Cerdà.[16] It is not a model that can be mapped onto other sites – which does not prevent the managers of other cities seeking to emulate its success.

More common are schemes such as the redevelopment of the harbour-side district of Bristol as a cultural quarter, with Arnolfini (art gallery), the Watershed (media centre) and a science theme park, At-Bristol, opened in July, 2000. The latter was described as 'a series of magnificent public squares and open spaces' with cafés and bars, spaces to relax, and public art.[17] The square, with French limestone paving, is also the roof of a car park (winning the Automobile Association Car Park Star Award in 2005), and the visual appearance of the site is close to that of the adjacent commercial space of the Lloyds Building. The artworks include bronze statues of white, male historical figures, deemed to be old Bristolians, including William Penn, Cary Grant, and the poet Thomas Chatterton. Chatterton died after taking a potion containing mercury, then a standard cure for sexually transmitted diseases. He is best known for fake medieval poetry, and his more original efforts found no publisher. I wonder what example he is supposed to set the young people of Bristol. Leaving that aside – an example of power's leakage, perhaps – my point is that the provision of new public squares is a distraction from other kinds of need including social mobility, justice, and democracy.[18] If such sites reflect a romanticized idea of the city, coloured by a sentiment that city air makes people free[19] (as if freedom is conjured out of air), or by idealized notions of life in the city-states of the Italian Renaissance, it is worth recalling that public spaces existed in such cities only outside monumental buildings while violent crime against the person flourished in the dark, narrow streets that led off them.[20] Today, new urban spaces of consumption are used by office workers and young professionals seeking respite from the pressures of flexible employment patterns,[21] and a new genre of aestheticized spaces feed the symbolic economies of cities competing globally.[22]

The new urban in the new world order

For sociologist Zygmunt Bauman, globalization means a fluidity of labour markets and mobility of production sites in a climate of de-regulation. It breeds new insecurities:

> Thrown into a vast open sea with no navigation charts and all the marker buoys sunk and barely visible, we have only two choices left: we may rejoice in the breath-taking vistas of new discoveries – or we may tremble out of fear of drowning. One opinion not really realistic is to claim sanctuary in a safe harbour.[23]

Bauman's pessimism is a matter of temperament, though he points to the increased mobility of a consuming elite, contrasted to greater controls on the movement of the poor as economic migrants and asylum seekers. Bauman also argues that the public realm is threatened by globalization, and sees a need to resist. Citing Habermas, he writes, 'The task [of critical theory] now is to defend the vanishing public realm, or rather to refurnish and repopulate the public space fast emptying owing to the desertion on both sides...'[24] of the engaged citizen and what he calls real power. The latter has migrated to 'the territory which...can only be described as "outer space"'[25] by which I think he means the de-centred spaces of global corporate restructuring, and probably cyberspace.

Several issues are conflated here which I want to unpack a little. First, there is a site of democratic interaction, or the supposition that one used to exist and is now being lost. A model for it is the Greek *agora* (market place) in which both goods and opinions were exchanged. In fact this was separate from the *pnyx* (assembly) in which political decisions were taken. The market was surrounded by food and drink stalls, and some administrative functions visited by the city's male property-owners. Yet political decisions not only took place in the assembly but were restricted to free men born in the city who owned a talent of silver (equivalent to 1,000 day's pay for a labourer). The proportion of the population allowed a political voice was thus about 5 per cent. But Bauman is not writing about Greece but laments the loss of capacity for political life in modern Europe. He expresses his response, however, in the vocabulary of a selective past as, 'to redesign and repopulate the now largely vacant agora – the site of meeting, debate and negotiation between the individual and the common, private and public good.'[26] Bauman echoes a dualism of public and private found previously in Hannah Arendt's work, in which the public is associated with freedom and the enclosed household with the restrictions of familiarity and patriarchy. Arendt writes that the term public means, 'that everything that appears in public can be seen and heard by everybody and has the widest possible publicity.'[27] This plots public light against private shade, and emphasizes the performativity of the public realm:

> Since our feeling for reality depends utterly upon appearances and therefore upon the existence of a public realm into which things can appear out of the darkness of sheltered existence, even the twilight which illuminates our private and intimate lives is ultimately derived from the much harsher light of the public realm.[28]

The performativity of Arendt's model informs Richard Sennett's discussion of the classical in *Flesh and Stone*,[29] where he juxtaposes outdoor, sunlit performances of masculinity to indoor, shaded performances of femininity. The distinction seems to inform the nineteenth century public realm; a set of men's spaces.

Another element of Arendt's argument is that the public realm is erased in mass culture.[30] Bauman, too, claims that the evacuation of the public realm is produced through the effects of mass culture, but sees a shift in the ground of the traditional dualism of public and private power and property when reassertions of privacy devalue common rights. He writes, 'Public power portends *incompleteness* of individual freedom, but its retreat or disappearance augurs the *practical impotence* of legally victorious freedom.'[31] If public regulation was a restriction of private property ownership and domestic life, the new difficulty is that public life is threatened by the repeal of regulation in the public interest. At the same time, Bauman argues, a new very public version of private life as celebrity-spectacle masks what he sees as the authentic concerns of society. I have compressed his argument, but Bauman echoes Adorno's view of mass culture as dulling public life.[32] He writes that television chat shows bring the private lives of celebrities to the public stage but reinforce the privacy in which publicly rehearsed dysfunctionalities are resolved in off-stage privacy:

> What is currently happening is not just another renegotiation of the notoriously mobile boundary between the private and the public...[It is] a redefinition of the public sphere, as a scene on which private dramas are staged.[33]

Bauman claims that celebrities and viewers renegotiate identity via a depoliticized consumerism so that, beside the first issue of democratic exchanges is a second of what might be called false exchanges, or exchanges limited to the terms of the market which deny the content of what would become a realm of political dialogue. This is contested by some sociologists investigating consumption as identity formation,[34] but coincides with Sharon Zukin's interpretation of consumer culture:

> Styles that develop on the streets are cycled through mass media...where, divorced from their social context, they become images of cool. On urban billboards advertizing designer perfumes or jeans, they are recycled to the streets, where they become a provocation, breeding imitation and even violence...The cacophony of demands for justice is translated into a coherent demand for jeans.[35]

This is the point. If a public sphere is a metaphorical site of social formation supporting and supported by individuals and groups in their formations of identity and autonomy, its issues are social equity and power and not the primacy of a brand of jeans; nor, in Bauman's terms, the resolution of love troubles or self-loathing among the rich. But this leads to a third issue, which is how to repopulate the emptied public realm or sphere – if there was one. My inclination is to question this on the grounds that, in ways apart from mass culture and the formal uses of public spaces, there remains diverse interaction between publics who contest the shape of the society. At times of revolt, or when power shifts, a repopulation of the public realm occurs in the destruction of monuments. But for the rest of the time, if in less obvious ways, specific publics identify common issues and claims (including claims to space). Specific, localized publics cross traditional class divides to produce as well as reflect models of cosmopolitanism. Annick Germain and Martha Radice argue, for example, that citizens' groups in Mile End, Montréal, during the gentrification of the area by young professionals, engaged in 'social issues such as getting a new library and reclaiming patches of spare land for much-needed parks,'[36] in the process linking Portuguese, Greek and Hassidic Jewish publics. This appears to be an incipient public sphere even though it does not yet translate into a political modality.

Sights and sites of public life

I said that I doubt the model of the Greek *agora* as a representation of a public, dialogic sphere. I have said, too, that the formal public spaces of metropolitan cities in Europe and north America – in which a plethora of statues appeared from the 1870s – constitute an exclusionary public realm. Grandiose architecture and embellishment in stone and bronze constitute the city as a series of vistas and distant views suggesting a coherence that denies the multiplicities of dwellers' lives. Doreen Massey writes, 'The privileging of vision impoverishes us through deprivation of other forms of sensory perception' through 'its supposed detachment.'[37] She sees that detachment not as Kantian disinterest but as a position of power: the universalizing overview, replicated in the conventional bird's eye (god's eye) viewpoint of the city plan. This is where official life takes place, or at least did until the effective evacuation of this public realm by the beneficial state in a period of de-regulation. As I say above, I think there are important questions arising from that; but the evacuation of monumental spaces is not in itself an evacuation of the locations of public life.

Where, then, does public life take place? Elizabeth Wilson writes that in Vienna before 1918, 'Public social life was important...The Corso section of the Ring saw the daily promenade of Viennese society, and the Viennese cafés were centres of intellectual discussion.'[38] The promenade was a largely bourgeois preoccupation; a performance of social status. But café life allowed a mixing of classes, and of migrants to the city. For Raymond Williams, the European avant-gardes of early Modernism occupied inter-class positions,[39] and were composed mainly of migrants to the cities which became hubs of new cultural work. As Williams also notes, 'within the very openness and complexity of the metropolis, there was no formed and settled society to which the new kinds of [cultural] work could be related.'[40] This added to the importance of transitional spaces, not quite public but not domestic either, such as the café in which groups of artists and writers met. In her study of European Bohemia, Wilson writes,

> Café culture was the consummation of the bohemians' love affair with urban life. They found there, or hoped to find, whatever had made them set out on their journey to Bohemia in the first place: the search for an enchanted way of life. The café was a chameleon environment, both hell and paradise...[41]

Few women were found in Viennese café society, and women promenading alone were assumed to be prostitutes but, nonetheless, accepting Wilson's criticism of conventional urban planning (that it denies women's right to excitement in the city),[42] her research on bohemian society shows that people who were strangers – immigrants or exiles,[43] or who transgressed sexual codes, survived as cultural producers by making common cause in such sites. In new cultural movements, identities were constructed through the extended perceptions of the self available amid the perceptions of others. This means the café is, in Arendt's terms, a location of publicity, the condition of mutual perception she regards as prerequisite for effective public life, the denial of which for Jews in Germany in the 1930s led to annihilation. Richard Lloyd notes, in a study of more recent music-based bohemias in north America, the significance of specific cafés – such as Urbus Orbis in Wicker Park, Chicago in the early 1990s – in enabling cultural sociation and contributing to the transformation of a neighbourhood: 'Urbus Orbis allowed for interactions that fostered a sense of community, and opportunities for mutual support and collaboration among aspiring cultural producers.'[44] Here is a difficulty in that the insertion of art cafés may aid gentrification. Yet it appears the café acts still as a quasi-public sphere for the interest-groups who use it. In many cases, frequenting a specific café is a way to belong to a sub-group within a cultural world. In a few cases there is a political dimension, as when Colonel Nasr and fellow officers met in a Cairo tea-house to plot the Egyptian Revolution of 1952. In England in the late seventeenth and early eighteenth centuries, too, political pamphlets circulated in men's clubs and coffee houses, contributing to the move to an incipient constitutional (if imported) monarchy in 1688.

If the café was important in Paris and Vienna, or in Chicago and San Francisco, in the Soviet period in the East-bloc it was in the kitchen that equivalent dialogic encounters occurred. Angela Harutyunyan writes of Armenia (a constituent republic of the Soviet Union until 1991), 'underground discussions were going on and alternative thought was formed; in the kitchen'.[45] The kitchen was outside surveillance, where people who knew each other and could, as it were, vouch for each other met to discuss matters of everyday life. Much of the discussion, if it was political, took obliquely critical forms, not least in jokes. These, as noted above, expressed an increasing cynicism about the regime. In a more detailed analysis specific to the Soviet Union's provision of shared apartments in ex-bourgeois blocks, the communal kitchen was a transitional space, neither public nor private. Looking at Leningrad, the city with the highest proportion of such apartments, Katerina Gerasimova notes, 'It might seem that the inhabitants of communal apartments were unaware that they lacked privacy, but the concept of privacy has never been a feature of Russian and Soviet culture and, in fact, the term itself is hard to translate into Russian.'[46] She insists that a western dichotomy of public and private cannot be mapped onto Russian society, and that life in such sites 'cannot be described as purely domestic or simply personal as it includes social relations with those who are neither members of the household nor of the family, and everyday life is regulated from outside.'[47]

To go a little further into the Soviet situation: after 1917, private ownership of property was abolished so that the home became part of the public sphere, regulated by the state. At the same time, the idea of private life, as a bourgeois institution, was opposed by a revolutionary allegiance to common life, at a time of collectivization. Since little new building was possible, new modes of housing such as the house-commune (which would have represented a non-private life) were not developed beyond the idea stage. A few house-communes were set up in existing buildings by young people 'living together as a single household, who pooled and redistributed their earnings...'[48] while, through the post-revolutionary period and into the 1930s a distinction was drawn between a counter-revolutionary privacy and an acceptable dimension of personal life. In the kitchens of communal apartments, then, people met in the queue for the bathroom or toilet, held comrades' courts, and encountered strangers.[49] In the 1960s, as state-socialism faced incursions of consumerism, especially in the German Democratic Republic, the home again became invested with values of security and withdrawal from the street. This was supported by the building of apartment blocks offering single-family units, usually on urban peripheries. Gerasimova argues that collective ideals remained, and,

> ...alternative public spheres based on friendship networks were formed at a time when the official public sphere was in crisis. Issues that should have been a matter of public concern... matters of culture and political events were often debated in private places. Moreover, the informal...economy was mostly based on immediate social and family connections and was, in some sense, private.[50]

This corresponds to Harutyunyan's remark on the kitchen. In both cases, domestic spaces are used by networks operating informal, non-money economies and exchanges of skills as well as ideas and critiques. The example of the Soviet kitchen is interesting not only in refuting a simple public-private dichotomy, then, but also as an incipient, performative public sphere. Perhaps, in present conditions, an incipient public sphere is as much as can be anticipated. The task, as it were, of critical theory is to recognize this rather than to attempt its theoretical definition. This, as I explain below, links to Lefebvre's idea of moments of presence that liberate awareness within, if also re-framing, the dulling routines of everyday life. Before returning to that, I want to emphasize the performative and ephemeral dimensions of a viable concept of a public sphere by looking at what happens in another kind of moment, that of revolt. For Lefebvre, in 1968, it may have seemed the two forms of moment coincided.

Rites of broken spaces

In periods of upheaval it becomes urgent for resistance to show the bankruptcy of the regime, and in the approach to such events for the regime to reaffirm itself, as in co-opting history. Sennett gives the example of Hadrian's inscription on the Pantheon of the name of a previous Emperor, Agrippa,[51] explaining that Hadrian felt dwarfed by his immediate predecessor, Trajan, and had murdered four Senators in his ascent to power. Seeking to shore up his legitimacy he appropriated public memory in using Agrippa's name, inscribing an image of a phoenix – emblem of Rome's revival under Augustus – on his coinage, too. In the nineteenth century, as imperial regimes faced threats to public order from anarchists and separatists, the commissioning of public monuments acted as such consolidation. In France after the defeat at Sedan in 1870 and consequent abdication of Napoleon III, rightist royalists and leftist republicans alike appropriated the imagery of Jean d'Orléans as a national symbol.[52] In Germany after its unification in the Wilhelmine period, medieval myths of Emperors Frederick (residing at Kyffhäusser in the Harz Mountains until his return) and Barbarossa (on the monument to Wilhelm I by Bruno Schmidtz, also at Kyffhäusser) were used to construct a back-story of invincibility.[53] This might loosely be compared with efforts by the Westminster regime today to invent notions of Britishness.

The new statuary provided a target for insurgents. In the Paris Commune in 1871, the 'Vendôme Column' – with a bronze statue of Napoleon I in Roman dress – was toppled. The event was organized by painter Gustave Courbet, whose first proposal was that the column be removed to storage (as manystatues of Lenin were in 1991). After the failure of the Commune, he was imprisoned but his main punishment was to be sent the bill – 323,091 Francs 68 centimes – for the monument's re-erection. My interest here, though, is in the rites of a enacting a shift of power. In this context, the toppling of the Vendôme Column was reported through eye-witness accounts in newspapers which reinterpret actions via past histories. Paul Wood cites an account stating, 'The column lies on the ground, split open...Caesar is lying prostrate and headless. The laurel wreathed head has rolled like a pumpkin into the gutter.'[54] A photograph taken the following day shows the statue intact.[55] The act of toppling was theatre on a grand public scale, referencing the fact that the open public space around the monument was used for military parades, and that Napoleon III was linked dynastically to Napoleon I. To be able to bring down the monument proved that power had shifted. The head may not have rolled away but spectators were able to kick it as if it was Napoleon himself.

Transitional spaces, transformative moments

A shift of power may lead to a replication of the monumental public realm in a new form. The question then is whether the model of power relations shifts in a shift of power. In Russia in 1917, after the destruction of the regime, Lenin's campaign of visual propaganda was informed by his reading of Campanella's *City of the Sun*, a sixteenth century text describing an ideal city in which knowledge is displayed in a sequence of public murals, to which children are taken for their education.[56] In the eighteenth century, Jean-Jacques Rousseau saw art, otherwise a corrupting luxury, as redeemed by such a role, as public information and instruction. Clearly, the public re-enactments of the revolution staged in Petrograd for its anniversaries were designed to impress the finality of the Revolution. They offered an opportunity for mass publics to re-enact the story, whether they had been there or not. Accounts of mass participation in the dismantling of the Berlin Wall in 1989 suggest some resonance with this, at the other end of the story, as well as with accounts of the violent abuse of statues of Stalin after his denunciation in the 1950s, or notably during the 1956 Hungarian uprising.[57] Sergiusz Michalski notes that a statue of Stalin in Budapest was dragged across the tramlines, broken up, beaten with poles, and used for 'especially vivid acts of public denigration.'[58] This recalls Place Vendôme in 1871. But perhaps, too, there are subtler ways in which the claims to power stated in monuments are resisted, undermined and dissolved by a refusal to invest in them the veneration required. For example, statues are sometimes given unofficial names – Marx and Lenin as' the pensioners'.

Yet I wonder if there is an extent to which public monuments, generally, are already hollow in meaning, erected after whatever they stand for has begun to lose currency. In a similar way, museums follow the demise of the categories their names state, so that museums of modern art, from New York to Tate Modern in London, date from the late 1920s to the 1990s while the period of experiment was from the 1890s to the 1910s, for which the anti-art of Dadaism from 1916 marks a termination. It can be noted that the Statue of Liberty was unveiled in 1882, the year in which a law was passed to limit the immigration of Chinese labourers to the United States.

In the Soviet Union under Brezhnev, the undermining of state power took the form of cynical humour. Since demolition of monuments was not possible, jokes proliferated on the regime's illusory grip on reality. For example: 'under Stalin, the train was on the tracks and went forward; under Kruschev it became necessary to remove the track from behind the train and place it in front so that it moved forwards; under Brezhnev, people on board the train acted as if it was moving.'[59] It is not funny. The punch-line denotes loss of belief in the system, which circulated with the rapidity of an agit-train. In Berlin after 1989, the graffiti *'Wir sind unschuldig'* ('we are innocent,) appeared on the plinth of the Marx-Engels Monument.[60] These quasi-jokes illustrate a latent resistance to power, produced in its interstices, and enhance the perception that representation of power is limited by the gap between abstract ideas such as nation and everyday life.

So, allegories appear contrived and use standard typologies as if almost anything can be represented. This applies to both old and new regimes, and the contest for an image of the Republic after the 1848 insurrection in Paris produced no notable art.[61]

In this context, Stephen Barber writes, in *Fragments of the European City*,

> The surfaces of the European city are strewn with grandiose and ambitious attempts to imprint nationality into them, to transmute the abstraction of nationality into visibility...But

the sheer tenuousness and intangibility of nationality...is projected by the silent fragments of its over-emphasis, its over-materialization. The national city is constructed from the heaviest, densest materials...The result is solid and static (the permanent representation of nation), but the vivid integral flux of the cities undermines and disintegrates that stasis...[62]

In contrast, liberation cannot be adequately represented in allegorical terms, though it might be conveyed in personal narratives of re-occupation or in shared cultural trends. Ana Betancour and Peter Hasdell write, for instance, of the agency of tango in Buenos Aires, contrasting the city's public spaces, 'modelled on the European, French and Anglo-Saxon ideals' with tango as 'part of the hidden or shameful world of the night' and which also represented a hybrid cultural identity and energy that 'threatened the hegemony of the official and authorized city.'[63] By contrasting popular occupations to official representations I do not mean that occupations are disorganized. I recall the solidarity of anti-war and anti-nuclear demonstrations in the 1960s. This cannot be reproduced. Nor, underneath, was the experience about changing policy as much as about being there among others of like mind. I think, speculatively because I was not there, that anti-road protests in the 1990s had a similar solidarity, and this is part of what Lefebvre means by a sense of presence, a kind of millenarianism in which rent is abolished in the landlord's lifetime, in which a new society is enacted.

Occupations are ephemeral but leave traces. They figure in public memory, and are an aspect of popular culture. While the representation of power in monuments is visual and static, occupation occurs in transitional and marginal sites, and crosses public and private spaces. To what extent, then, are those involved aware of either the historical significance or the mutuality of the re-framing of a society that takes place? Ali Madanipour compares two perceptions of city crowds in the late nineteenth century: for Friedrich Engels they are atomistic – the individuals in them have no connection; yet for Edward Ashworth Ross, in 1908, 'A condition of order at the junction of crowded city thoroughfares implies primarily an absence of collision...the throng is *orderly*.' [64] [original italics] This suggests occupation is not disorganized; or, acts of spatial occupation have an intrinsic if seemingly spontaneous order. The actors have no script, but a vocabulary of possible ways of seeing, doing and speaking. Another way to put this is, from Catherine Belsey, that culture constitutes 'the vocabulary within which we do what we do; it specifies the meanings we set out to inhabit or repudiate, the values we make efforts to live by or protest against...'[65] while the protest, as she adds, is also cultural. This does not mean spontaneous action is the forerunner of institutionalization, as if social groups only re-enact past patterns of sociation or power. Madanipour objects to this dramaturgical model, in which 'all social behaviour is potentially performing,'[66] but in which there is a tacit assumption that actors cannot exchange masks. On the public sphere, he adds,

It refers to both the state and the society, both to their entirety and their subscriptions, both to universal and particular categories, both to impersonal and interpersonal relations, both to concrete and abstract concepts, both to normative and descriptive notions, and to many shades of publicness, where degrees of access, interest and agency vary widely.[67]

Lived space, lived time

Perhaps a viable model for a public sphere is an axis of creative tension between the public, the private (or domestic), and the personal. David Crowley writes of life in Warsaw in the Soviet era, 'it is not difficult to conceive the private space of the home as a place of escape from a cheerless environment and from ethical compromises.'[68] He cites writer Czeslaw Milosz that intellectuals were prepared to write propaganda to protect their freedom in private spaces inhabited through state allocation. Crowley summarizes, 'public acts of faith secured private freedoms. In this vein, the private home...was understood as being the limit of intrusions from the public sphere.'[69] A private apartment or domestic space such as the kitchen may in some conditions be where a politicized social life occurs. In contrast, the public spaces of a city, or its work spaces, might be more under surveillance (or the gaze of a monumental realm). At this point, the idea of a public sphere becomes tenuous, denoting a range of partial interactions or ephemeral instants of accord, or discord, distributed throughout the world of everyday life. In terms of Lefebvre's theory of space, the public sphere is aligned to spaces of occupation, which Lefebvre calls lived spaces in distinction from the conceived spaces of plans, elevations, geometries and regulations.[70] The latter is the product of a Cartesian system, using its coordinates to conjure a seamless, universal space (or quality of space) in which all is ordered and predictable. It is not surprising that this realm of order grew from Descartes' struggle with doubt. And doubt is in a way sedimented in its geometry. Lived spaces, in contrast, are plural sites of human occupation, tending to interrupt planned space, or appropriate part of it for other than the designated purpose – given that planned space tends to functionalism and zoning. Lefebvre notes that those who occupy spaces are termed users, so that 'Their marginalization by spatial practice thus extends even to language.'[71] But this space is also concrete, material – it exists. Seeing a conflict between the privacy of lived spaces and the public realm of conceived space, Lefebvre adds that there is another gap between the ephemeral and the stable, arguing that a space inhabited by subjects might be called relational. This also means a restoration of the multi-sensual:

> The restoration of the body means...the restoration of the sensory-sensual...of the non-visual. And of the sexual...in the sense of a sexual energy...flowing according to specific rhythms.[72]

This might be called libido, and there is a Utopian tradition of the libidinal society as elaborated by Charles Fourier in the nineteenth century, where work is eroticized as social relations among people of sympathetic disposition. When Marcuse's essay on French literature under the German occupation[73] – in which the last resort of freedom is in a literature of intimacy – is read in this context it accords with Fourier and the passage from Lefebvre cited above in an imagined libidinal and ludic society.

If that is a Utopian idea, and Utopianism tends to look to a future which never dawns but remains a dream (though it has a practical side, too), the task of critical theory emerges clearly. It is not so much to repopulate the public realm or invest it with radical democracy, though that may also happen, but to recognize the liberated in the midst of ordinary life. This brings me finally to Lefebvre's theory of moments – which I now read as a speculative definition of a public sphere. But what are these moments, or moments of presence within the routines of everyday lives, in which a sudden but lasting and transformative clarity appears? Rob Shields summarizes, 'Moments outflank the pretensions of wordy theories, rules and laws, and challenge the limits of everyday living...a sudden insight into a situation or an experience beyond the merely empirical routine of some activity.'[74] The moment thus intersects public and private spaces, re-frames public realms, may occur during acts of revolt or in intimacy, and remains indefinable.

In the second volume of *Critique of Everyday Life*, Lefebvre differentiates between the terms 'moment' and 'instant'. He writes that while instants are ephemeral, and no more than that, moments linger within the histories of individuals (whose lives 'cannot be separated from the social sphere'[75]) and take a number of forms. Moments of presence occur within everyday life, deriving their content from it but transforming it – '[the moment] uses something it is not: something happening close by, something contingent and accidental.'[76] Then, Lefebvre defines the moment as an attempt to fully realize potential – the potential of a life which is becoming – and which is in the act the beginning of that realization. Going through various philosophical categories, ensuring that the moment both fits them and does not, he writes,

> If we must fit the theory of moments into some kind of classification, we will say that it has a contribution to make to an *anthropology*, but with two provisos: first that we do not confuse this anthropology with a culturalism..., and second that we do not omit radical critique of all specializations, including anthropology.[77]

In short, because I cannot go fully into this highly enigmatic and elusive concept here, the moment enables everyday experiences to be more than trivial or routine, almost like an embedded critical distance, going beyond the confusions of spontaneous life towards an intrinsic, immanent order between nature and culture. The final word of the volume is 'Festival'.[78]

By way of a coda, I cite a text produced by Freee Art Collective (Mel Jordan, Andy Hewitt and Dave Beech), from an exhibition of billboard and text works:

> The concept of public space, beloved of lonely myopic law-abiding right-on gushing morons, can only imagine the public as a mass of bodies.

> The concept of the public realm, preferred by shifty piss-guzzling half-witted busy-body nerve-wracked self-serving technocrats, can only imagine the public as a mass to be administered.

> The concept of a public sphere, in the radical tradition of Critical Theory, imagines the public producing itself through politicized acts of cultural exchange.[79]

Malcolm Miles is Professor of Cultural Theory at the University of Plymouth, and author of Urban Utopias *(2008) and* Urban Avant-Gardes *(2004).*

Notes

1. Figes, O. (1997) *A People's Tragedy: The Russian Revolution 1891–1924*. London, Pimilco, pp. 40–41; Figes notes the possibility that, had the liberal reformists of the 1860s and 1870s not been displaced after Alexander II's assassination, Russia 'might have become a Western-style society based upon individual property...' p. 40.
2. Bloch, E. (1986) *The Principle of Hope*. Cambridge, Mass, MIT, pp. 509–515 on Joachim of Fiore.
3. Didion, J. (2001) 'Slouching Towards Bethlehem', in *Slouching Towards Bethlehem*. London, Flamingo, p. 72 [essay first published, Los Angeles, *The Saturday Evening Post*, 1967; collection first published New York, Farrar, Strauss and Giroux, 1968].
4. Dürrschmidt, J. (1999)'the Local Versus the Global? Individual Milieux in a Complex risk Society: the Case of Organic Food Box schemes in the South-West', in Hearn, J and Roseneil, S, eds, *Consuming Cultures: Power and Resistance*. Basingstoke, Macmillan, pp. 131–154.
5. Figes, O. (1997) *A People's Tragedy: The Russian Revolution 1891–1924*. London, Pimilco, p. 162; see also Carr, E.H. (1966) *The Bolshevik Revolution, 1917–23*, vol. 1, Harmondsworth, Penguin. Carr argues that Marxism gained acceptance in the 1890s 'due to the expansion of Russian industry and to the absence of any bourgeois tradition or bourgeois political philosophy which could play in rissia the role of western liberalism.' (p. 21).
6. Lefebvre, H. (2008) *The Critique of Everyday Life* vol. 2, London, Verso, Ch. 6.
7. Lefebvre, H. (1991) *The Production of Space*. Oxford, Blackwell.
8. Soja, E. (1996) *Thirdspace: Journeys to Los Angeles and other real-imagined places*. Oxford, Blackwell.
9. Marcuse, H. (1968) 'Liberation from the Affluent Society', in Cooper, D., ed., *the Dialectics of Liberation*. Harmondsworth, Penguin, p. 185; Marcuse, H. (2007) 'Society as a Work of Art', in Marcuse, H., *Art and Liberation*, Collected Papers vol. 4, London, Routledge, pp. 123–129.
10. Miles, M. (2004) *Urban Avant-Gardes: Art, Architecture and Change*. London, Routledge, pp. 71–80.
11. Bloch, E. *The Principle of Hope*. Cambridge, Mass, MIT; Adorno, T. W. and Horkheimer, M. (1997) *Dialectic of Enlightenment*. London, Verso; Marcuse, H. (1967) *Reason and Revolution*. London, Routledge & Kegan Paul.
12. Marcuse, H. (1969) *An essay on Liberation*. Harmondsworth, Penguin, p. 10.
13. During a workshop on urban spaces and cultures organised by the School of Geography at the Open University in 2005, in Milton Keynes, I observed groups of up to a dozen or so young people using the central space, around an indoor oak tree, of the mall for hanging out. When consumption took place it tended that one person would buy a soft drink or ice cream and share it. This enabled them to use the chairs, offering ringside seats on the sociation of others, at minimum cost; see also Miles, S. (2003) 'Resistance or Security? Young people and the appropriation of urban cultural and consumer spaces', in Miles, M. and Hall, T., eds (2003) *Urban Futures: critical essays on shaping the city*. London, Routledge, pp. 65–75.
14. Designed by Carme Fiol Costa (1988–89); see Gozalez, A. and Lacuesta, R. (2002) *Barcelona architecture guide 1929–2002*. Barcelona, Editorial Gili, p. 110.
15. Dodd, D. (1999) 'Barcelona: the Making of a Cultural City', in Dodd. D. and van Hemel, A., eds *Planning Cultural Tourism in Europe: A Presentation of Theories and Cases*. Amsterdam, Boeckmann Stichting, pp. 53–64.
16. Miles, M. (2007) *Cities and Cultures*. London, Routledge, pp. 87–88, 93–94.
17. www.at-bristol.org.uk/open/default.htm [accessed 16 October, 2007.
18. Loftman, P. and Nevin, B. 'Prestige Projects, City-Centre Restructuring and Social Exclusion: Tackling the Long-Term View', in Miles, M. and Hall, T., eds *Urban Futures: critical essays on shaping the city*, pp. 76–91.

19. This references the sign at gates to cities of the medieval Hanseatic League, around the Batic Sea; see Sennett, R. (2000) *Flesh and Stone*, p. 155; Soja, E. *Postmetropolis: Critical Studies of Cities and Regions*. Oxford, Blackwell, p. 248.

20. Sennett, R. (2003) *Flesh and Stone*, London: Penguin, p. 196.

21. Sennett, R. (1998) *The Corrosion of Character: The Personal Consequences of Work in the New Capitalism*. New York, Norton.

22. Zukin, S. (1995) *The Cultures of Cities*. Oxford, Blackwell.

23. Bauman Z. (1998) *Globalization: the Human Consequences*. Cambridge, Polity, p. 85.

24. Bauman, Z. (2000) *Liquid Modernity* Cambridge, Polity, p. 39.

25. Ibid.

26. Bauman , Z (2000) *Liquid Modernity*. Cambridge, Polity, p. 41.

27. Arendt, H. (1958) *The Human Condition*. Chicago, University of Chicago Press, p. 50.

28. Ibid, p. 51.

29. Sennett, *Flesh and Stone*, London: Penguin, pp. 31–123.

30. Arendt, H. (1958) *The Human Condition*. Chicago, University of Chicago Press, pp. 58–60.

31. Bauman, Z (2000) *Liquid Modernity*. Cambridge, Polity, p. 51.

32. For examples: Adorno, T. W. (1991) *The Culture Industry: Selected essays on mass culture*. London, Routledge; Adorno, T. W. (1994) *The Stars Down to Earth and other essays on the Irrational in Culture*. London, Routledge.

33. Bauman, Z (2000) *Liquid Modernity*. Cambridge, Polity, p. 70.

34. For example, Nava, M. (1992) *Changing Cultures: Feminism, Youth and Consumerism*. London, Sage.

35. Zukin S. (1995) *The Cultures of Cities*. Oxford, Blackwell, p. 9.

36. Germain, A. and Radice, M. (2006) 'Cosmopolitanism by Default: public sociability in Montréal', in Binnie, J., Holloway, J., Millington, S. and Young, C., eds, *Cosmopolitan Urbanism*. London, Routledge, pp. 112–129.

37. Massey, D. (1994) *Space, Place and Gender*. Cambridge, Polity, p. 232.

38. Wilson , E. (1991) *The Sphinx in the City: Urban Life, the Control of Desire, and Women* Berkeley, University of California Press, p. 84.

39. Williams, R. (1996) *The Politics of Modernism*. London, Verso, p. 54.

40. Ibid, p. 46.

41. Wilson, E. (2003) *Bohemians: The Glamorous Outcasts*. London, Tauris Parke, p. 34.

42. Wilson, E. (1991) *The Sphinx in the City: Urban Life, the Control of Desire, and Women*. Berkeley, University of California Press, pp. 135–159.

43. See also Williams, *The Politics of Modernism*, pp. 37–48.

44. Lloyd, R. (2006) *Neo-Bohemia: art and commerce in the postindustrial city*. New York, Routledge, p. 109.

45. Harutyunyan, A. (2003) 'Public Media Space', project leaflet (Yerevan, Centre for Contemporary Experimental Art) [not paginated].

46. Gerasimova, K. (2002) 'Public Privacy in the Soviet Communal Apartment', in Crowley, D. and Reid, S. E., eds *Socialist Spaces: Sites of Everyday Life in the Eastern Bloc*. Oxford, Berg, p. 207.

47. Ibid, p. 208.

48. Ibid, p. 209.

49. Ibid, p. 217.

50. Ibid, p. 210.

51. Sennett , *Flesh and Stone*, p. 92.
52. Warner, M. (1981) *Joan of Arc: The Image of Female Heroism*. London, Weidenfeld and Nicholson.
53. Michalski, S. (1998) *Public Monuments: Art in Political Bondage 1870–1997*. London, Reaktion, pp. 62–63.
54. In Edwards, S., ed. (1973) *The Communards of Paris, 1871*. London, Thames and Hudson, pp. 147–148; cited in Wood, P. ed. (1999) *The Challenge of the avant-Garde*. New Haven, Yale University Press, p. 119.
55. Roth, M. S., with Lyons, C. and Merewether, C. (1997) *Irresistible Decay*. Los Angeles, Ghetty Research Institute for the History of Art and the Humanities, p. 14, fig. 8 [albumen print by Bruno Braquehais, 1871].
56. Bown, M. C. and Tayklor, B., eds (1993) *Art of the Soviets: Painting, Sculpture and Architecture in a One-Party State, 1917–1992*. Manchester, Manchester University Press, pp. 16–33; see also Tolstoy, V., Bibikova, I., and Cooke, C. (1990) *Street Art of the Russian Revolution*. New York, Vendome Press).
57. Michalski, S. (1998) *Public Monuments: Art in Political Bondage 1870–1997*. London, Reaktion, pp. 138–153.
58. Ibid, p. 141.
59. Conversation with Vardan Azatyan, 16 October, 2007.
60. Michalski, S. (1998) *Public Monuments: Art in Political Bondage 1870–1997*. London, Reaktion, p. 147 (Fig. 99).
61. Clark T. J. (1973) *The Absolute Bourgeois: Artists and Politics in France 1848–1851*. London, Thames and Hudson.
62. Barber, S. (1995) *Fragments of the European City* (London, Reaktion, p. 51.
63. Betancour, A. and Hasdell, P. 'Tango: A choreography of urban displacement', in Lokko, L. N. N., ed. *White Papers, Black Marks: Architecture, Race, Culture*. London, Athlone, 2000) pp. 146–175.
64. In Madanipour, A. (2003) *Public and Private Spaces of the City*. London, Routledge, p. 114.
65. Belsey, C. (2001) *Shakespeare and the Loss of Eden*. Basingstoke, Palgrave, p. 7.
66. Madanipour, A. (2003) *Public and Private Spaces of the City*. London, Routledge, p. 130.
67. Ibid, p. 134.
68. Crowley, D. 'Warsaw Interiors: The Public Life of Private Spaces, 1949–1965', in Crowley, D. and Reid, S., eds *Socialist Spaces: Sites f everyday life in the Eastern bloc*, Berg, p. 187.
69. Ibid.
70. Lefebvre, H. (1991) *The Production of Space*. Oxford, Blackwell, p. 317, 361.
71. Ibid, p. 362.
72. Ibid, p. 363.
73. Marcuse, H. (1998) 'Some Remarks on Aragon: Art and Politics in the Totalitarian Era', in *Technology, War and Fascism*. London, Routledge, pp. 199–214.
74. Shields, R. (1999) *Lefebvre, Love and Struggle*. London, Routledge, p. 58.
75. Lefebvre, H. (2008) *Critique of everyday Life*, vol. 2, London, Verso, p. 344.
76. Ibid, p. 346.
77. Ibid, p. 350.
78. Ibid, p. 358.
79. Freee Art Collective, 'How to Make a Difference' exhibition catalogue (Birmingham, Bournville Centre for Visual Arts, 2007) [not paginated].

intellect books

Art & Theory
After Socialism

art & design

Art and Theory After Socialism

Edited by Mel Jordan, Malcolm Miles

ISBN 9781841502113/ £19.95 / $40

Contemporary visual culture, art, theory and criticism shifted after the end of the Cold War, so that cultural production in both the East and the West underwent radical new challenges. *Art and Theory After Socialism* considers the new critical insights that are produced in the collisions of art theory from the ex-East and ex-West. The collected essays assert that dreams promised by consumerism and capitalism have not been delivered in the East, and that the West is not a zone of liberation, increasingly drawn into global conflict as well as media presentation of a high-risk society.

For other related titles go to
www.intellectbooks.com

intellect publishers of original thinking

The Mill, Parnall Road, Bristol BS16 3JG 0117 9589910 www.intellectbooks.com